D0943955

THE MOUNTAINS OF
MY LIFE

The Nuvolao Traverse. Torre Grande: a Dolomite Grade III. climb

THE MOUNTAINS OF MY LIFE

Journeys in Turkey and the Alps

By

ASHENDEN

WILLIAM BLACKWOOD & SONS LTD
EDINBURGH AND LONDON
1954

To the Ballianis

whose welcoming home was the gateway to my first hills,

And to Perry

whose awareness brought warmth to the middle years.

CONTENTS

LIST OF ILLUSTRATIONS

ix

LIST OF ILLUSTRATIONS

FOREWORD

THIS is a book about the hills ; except for the chapter called " Journey to Hierapolis," where I write of the trials and humour of Anatolian travel, it deals mainly with my mountain memories, starting with earliest years and continuing to beyond the milepost of my third decade.

It can hardly be considered a text-book for climbers. The technical expert may find little to interest him in the writings of one whose capacities as a cragsman are clearly limited. I have not had the opportunity to meet fellow-mountaineers, or enjoyed the company of persons of an equal mind, except rarely. But I hope my book will interest some people, and give pleasure to those who enjoy travelling and appreciate the mountain scene.

Inevitably my outlook differs a good deal from that of the " Moderns." I am as content to walk the hills as to climb, and find much of the happiness of the mountains linked to the idea of a voyage—to new horizons and starry skies, and the sense of liberation in wide spaces.

The chapters that follow are varied both in scope and in mood. Some describe a single incident or adventure, others a whole series of impressions and events. Starting with gentle days spent in the romance of youth, they end with the more sober view and sterner enterprises of middle years· I have come to write them mainly to bring to memory again the good times of the first three decades of my life, and to re-create the pleasures and the adventures of my mountain days : at the same time I have tried to communicate something of the message of the hills.

It seems better to write while the impressions are vivid and close, rather than await the detachment of later years ; for age stands on a watershed and views the events in the valley through long, mysterious perspectives. One can scarcely be said even to have approached the watershed at thirty-two, but already I feel planted on a certain eminence, from which the incidents in the lower valley begin to blur ; and the vision upward towards the heights is cloudy, for the days we live in are uncertain.

I have to thank the Editor of ' Blackwood's ' for allowing me to include in this book some material that has already appeared in his Magazine.

MODA,   *September* 1953.
ISTANBUL.

CHAPTER I

BOURNABAT—A ROMANCE OF SPRING

OUR house near Istanbul looked across the waters of the Sea of Marmora, over the gentle lines of the Princes' Islands, towards the long silhouette of the Argonthonius Range, and beyond, on clear days, to the snows of the Bithynian Olympus. This fair view has remained with me all my life. And years of exile from it, at school in England or on the harsh plateau of Anatolia, have only served to print it more deeply upon the mind. I have always returned to it with relief, and with unlessened feeling. Amid the shifting currents of life it is one of the few things that has, for me, stability.

Of my earliest childhood memories none is more clear than the memory of constant aspiration towards the blue line of the Argonthonius Range. Those mountain shapes, softened by the thirty miles of their distance, seemed to hold the key to felicity, the door to some enchanted, unattainable kingdom. And the current of feeling which was then set flowing has continued through the decades, and will, I hope, sustain me to the end. For, on the whole, mountaineers are born, not made. There is a certain fatality in their mould, which is set firm at birth. The emotions of some men can be deflected to many ends, but the affective stream of the mountaineer remains flowing steadily in its channel.

When I was very young my father used to hire a house-boat called the *KEF*, on which we would spend the summer holidays cruising in the coastal waters of the Marmora, past the Princes' Islands and Mavri Island, and the monastery-topped, craggy shape of Andreas Island. These are ancient, historical waters, blessed by warm winds in summer, and deepened to a rich blue under the *meltem*, the steady north-east breeze. My father was a yachtsman at heart and taught us many things about the sea. We learnt how to swim and fish, how to look after a rowing-boat and hoist a lateen sail, how to make camp and be competent in weather-lore. Whenever we went to Andreas Island, or Monastiraki Beach, my pleasure mounted because from these places the blue line of the mountains was closer, and one could see the forested fur of the ridges and the shade of profound valleys. One memorable day the old *KEF* was persuaded to venture out to Tuzla Point—a mere fifteen miles from the mountains, and I almost fainted from excitement when my father decided to try for the opposite coast. The moment, about half an hour later, when the freshening waves made us turn back just when I thought the Blue Mountains were within my reach, has remained fixed in memory as the first bitter disappointment of life.

The Blue Mountains of childhood have long since given up their secrets, and the Argonthonius peninsula is now a place of pleasaunce for the week-ends of summer. But starting from that early ambition my steps have been carried steadily on by the affective stream, which met every parental opposition and set-back with a cautious tenacity. For more than fifteen years the stream flowed underground—pent in by the enclosing walls of illness or the necessities of wartime or schooling. Only after I was twenty-five did the hills suddenly leap into daylight again and become accessible. Then I turned to the gracious summits of Smyrna, and

2

continued onwards, past my first sight of the Upper World on the Bithynian Olympus, to one of the final goals of the hillsman—the Pennine Alps of Switzerland. The rock peaks of the Ala Dağ Taurus followed, and the Dolomites ; then again the Zermatt giants. But that is all by way of anticipation.

II

I have written of Istanbul because it was my birthplace, but it is the village of Bournabat, near Smyrna, which has perhaps had the greatest influence on my life and tastes as a wayfarer.

Bournabat was the home of my maternal grandmother and the centre of a great, though vanishing, tradition in living. In a sense it did not quite belong to this world ; for the people who lived there existed in a kind of enchanted microcosm, recalling the Shangri La of a modern novel. Generations of ancient families like the Whittalls, Girauds, and La Fontaines (my mother was a La Fontaine) had lived out their lives in patriarchal peace and prosperity within its shadowed gardens. They had intermarried among themselves and other foreign families to produce a multi-lingual, multi-national community which had lived together with extraordinary compactness and intimacy for over a hundred years. Practically everyone was a close relative of his neighbour. The only sort of social conventions which obtained were those you would expect in a family circle. Eccentricity and strongly marked personality were the rule, and the dividing line between youth and age and nationality and nationality was practically non-existent. There was great

3

frankness of speech. A French newcomer to the community once told my cousin Audrey : " *Tu es tellement franche que ça frise la bêtise,*" and immediately received the laughing reply, " *Toi tu es tellement diplomate que ça frise l'Hypocrisie* " —which typifies to a certain extent what was thought of outsiders and outside conventions.

Entering Bournabat gave to a member of the family the sensation of being compassed about by a great cloud of feeling, by all the intimacy of a home, flowing towards one with a kind of solidity and warmth of comfort ; but a home spread over a whole community instead of being confined to a single house. In the period up to the First World War the Bournabat community enjoyed wealth and material ease of life. Great homes were constructed, and fine gardens, in the romantic tradition of Italy, were laid out. The period produced immensely numerous families, and men and women of outstanding character. My great grandmother, Magdalen Whittall, who ruled supreme over the village like a Biblical matriarch, lived to see five generations of her family alive at the same time, and had 256 direct descendants when she died. Some of my maternal forebears amassed important collections of rugs and *objets d'art*. Others were devoted to water-colour painting or to their properties. And one of them was so wrapped up in his plants and trees that he neglected every other occupation in life except the creation of beauty in his garden. Many of the family were noted wits, and the last of these died in recent times ; throughout his final ten years of illness his tongue and his pen poured out a stream of epigrams, mocking verse and repartee in three languages, which scintillated but never stabbed.

The period of material splendour closed in 1922, when the

great houses and properties were sacked in the Smyrna fire, and the old way of things came irrevocably to an end. But somehow the spirit of ease in life, the gaiety and the warmth of feeling lingered on, to survive all material set-backs. The ancestral properties slowly mouldered to rest. The houses acquired the sadness and charm of decaying things. Perhaps in their declining years, when the guardian cypresses had become giants of wood and foliage towering over a hundred feet into the sky, those ancient demesnes held more romance within their walls than during their younger days. The high stone boundaries round each property conferred a feeling of seclusion. The cypresses murmuring drowsily in the breeze gave peace. And the mountains looking down on Bournabat from three sides added a sense of changelessness and stability.

From the first, Bournabat was associated in my mind with the idea of a voyage and all the thrill of foreign lands. Before we went to school in England my sister and I made infrequent visits with my mother to the old family house in Bournabat. The thirty-six hour boat journey and the prospect of going to Grannie Blanche's would keep me in a state of excitement for weeks before. Life at our home in Istanbul seemed so insulated from danger and exposure to nature that Smyrna, with its impression of greater wildness, always beckoned with the allure of adventure.

The whole world of nature was closer in Bournabat, more vehement and active. It was an exotic world with the warmth of southern places in its air. From the ranks of the cypresses in the day would come the cooing of innumerable pigeons, and at night from my grandmother's house one could hear the jackals calling in the hills ; mingling with this, the hooting of owls and the rattle of frogs from the marsh would

5

Gathering storm : the Hills of Papazyan, near Bournabat

come winging across the darkness into my room through the slats of the shutters. The animal life was different in Smyrna. There were chameleons and black scorpions. The lizards that sunned themselves on the rocky walls by the olive trees were spiky and toughly carapaced like mythological dragons. I used to stalk them with a catapult, feeling much the same trepidation as a man hunting a rhinoceros.

The rains would descend with violence, and then one heard the thunder of the torrent of " Chai " which came down from the Lake Tantalus Mountains. In times of extreme downpour, the grinding of the boulders being hurtled along its bed by the force of the water would make even grown-up people quail. One fatal year the torrent broke its banks and sent the raging red waters and their cargo of boulders rushing through the village. I used to watch the Chai in fascination from the bridge, and noticed how smoothly rounded were all the stones and boulders on the walls of Bournabat.

It was this proximity to the things of nature, as I saw them then, which gave to Bournabat a great deal of its charm. The biggest attraction, though, was the nearness of the mountains. Just behind the village the Lake Tantalus range reared its wooded slopes, and across the Smyrna Plain rose the heavy five-thousand-foot wall of the Nimph Dağ, immeasurably high and impressive, with every detail visible. I could see the individual trees and rocks. It was no distant, unattainable aspiration, this, like the Argonthonius range from Istanbul, but a flesh-and-blood mountain—the first real mountain love of my life. I decided that as soon as I was old enough I would make my way across the plain and mount the complicated buttresses that led to its crown of final rocks.

6

I could not then conceive of any joy more perfect than to attain the summit of the Nimph Dağ.

III

More than a decade was to go by before I saw Bournabat again. Much had altered. The years at an English prep. school and at Rugby were behind me. My grandmother was dead. The property was sold. And the war had been on for a year and a half. I had come to man's estate, but the mountains were still as far away as ever, for illness had greatly restricted my powers of movement, and was to keep me even from office work for seventeen months. Repeated attacks of pneumonia in my schooldays (before the advent of sulfa drugs and penicillin) had bequeathed me an impaired right lung; and hepatic troubles of a serious nature were afterwards to leave me crippled throughout many years.

It was now the winter of 1941, and I arrived one January evening to stay at my Aunt Clara's house for a period of convalescence. This was the first real voyage of my life in the sense that it was undertaken voluntarily, and with adult faculties responding to impressions with the full intensity of youth.

Istanbul had been left in sleet and murk, but in Bournabat it was already a different world. I felt a sudden shedding of many worries and pangs. The past fell silently away; the smooth-slipping years receded, until, like the opening of light at the end of a tunnel which reveals a different valley, the ancient, forgotten Bournabat of childhood flowed quietly back to consciousness. I climbed up the stairs to my room, and in darkness walked across to its window. Opening the

7

shutters I looked out, striving to pierce the blackness of the night and discern the high silhouette of the Nimph Dağ. But the only things that met the eye were two forms of cypress that stood cold and immutable, imposing upon the stillness of the night a kind of grandeur, charged with mystery. Against the intensity of their blackness the sky seemed to pale into the semblance of a wan daylight ; and the night, though clouded, was soft and drowsy, while the air that stirred the great trees into a murmurous rustle and swish was itself full of balm, and perfumed with the fragrance of half-forgotten, magical scents that brought thronging back a thousand vanished memories. I remember this night as one of the signal occasions of life, and later experience has confirmed me in the belief that pleasures and impressions depend largely for their intensity upon rarity. The sharpest emotions stem from unique occasions, and the more you do a thing, the less it comes to mean.

The next day the sun was streaming through the pines and cypresses and casting, through the open slats of the shutters, a latticed image of morning and warmth into the room.

When I walked into the square from Aunt Clara's I was met by a host of spires that rose up in all directions—no ordinary spires, but lofty, tapering forms of the richest and darkest green. A delight rose up in me at seeing the cypresses that brood in calm and changeless majesty over the old homes and gardens which lie beneath. The whole scene diffused an air of surpassing tranquillity. It was a peace fragrant with a multitude of soft and indefinable scents that permeated the atmosphere and gave it an intangible sensuousness. There was something rich and strange in the sight of

8

so much evergreen, and in a warmth so unnatural for the middle of January.

The birds and the plants and all the realm of nature seemed here to be spared the barrenness and stern frigidity of winter. It was not really spring that stirred the air, but only an absence of harshness. The season was winter, but winter shorn of all her normal accompaniments and lying dormant.

I gazed at the mountains from whose presence the place derives so much of its enchantment. They say that Bournabat would not be Bournabat without its cypresses : but still less so without the mountains that surround it on three sides— never obtrusive, sometimes nearer, sometimes farther—and always gazing down on the transitoriness that lies below them with the ageless dignity of high places.

I spent many days in a small folding chair on a hillock in Harry Giraud's property, called the Kiosk. To the left across the plain lay the Nimph Dağ. To the right, in the west, the twin volcanic peaks of the Two Brothers poised themselves delicately above the Gulf of Smyrna. In those days of ceaseless gazing with the Zeiss glasses, I learnt much about the fleeting moods of the hills, and began to make judgments by small, almost indiscernible scraps of evidence, with past reading for a background, about such things as weather and atmosphere. Sometimes the essence of travelling can be instilled into a life that never stirs from its home, and the most perfect voyages undertaken with the imagination only for a guide.

Days on the Kiosk were sometimes interrupted by storms and cold. Not all the winter was mild. Sometimes the north winds would roar down from the Lake Tantalus Mountains, bearing their train of sleet and cold. And the pleasure would change to that of lying in bed in my little room and listening to the creak of the boughs, and the thunder of the gale, as it bent before it the cypresses outside my window. The air would be bitter and acrid with the clean scent of cold and snow, and the mountains would stand gleaming in virginal whiteness.

Well into March their higher reaches kept this garb, but when the first gust of heat came there was a sudden pause—a quivering, and the whole place gave itself anew to the activity of birth.

On those first days of spring, when the air was no more full of balm, but scattered and shimmering in the voluptuousness of heat and the promise of summer, one could sense the nascent effort of all growing things. Wandering round the dark, mysterious lanes of Bournabat at night, I could almost hear a muffled crepitation, as of the seething and swarming of new cells, of sap rising and the rapid burgeoning of leaf and shoot.

Those spring nights remain graven in the mind as a series of memories almost dream-like in their otherworldly quality. The beauty was less one of form than of atmosphere and scent. The air was filled with troubling fragrance : no longer soft and indefinable odours, but the full, rich perfumes of orange-blossom and wistaria, of mimosa and tuberose and ambéri, which so filled the night that one was ever conscious of the heady richness of one or another. The air was warm, yet refreshing to the skin as water to a swimmer.

When I began to get a little stronger, some of my best hours were spent among the shallow hills of Papazyan's, just outside Bournabat, or at the Red Field, where during the season the whole earth seemed to flame with untold legions of anemones. The slopes were covered with wild asphodel and oleander. Often, while lying flat on some little rise looking down the enchanted view to the Two Brothers, I would catch the clean, aromatic smell of the mountain herbs wafted up from the earth and experience a strange sense of one-ness with the world of hills and plants. Bournabat lay below embowered in its cypresses. The horizon was a far and beckoning line, and the whole world seemed to be man's heritage. I felt like Ulysses questing to sail beyond the sunset and the baths of all the western stars.

When the time came to leave Bournabat I realised that I would never again be content to live without some hope in the future—however remote—of renewed experience in travel, of mountains to climb, of places to visit, whose beauty my heart would respond to. For a definite pattern of tastes and longings had been evoked. Unfadable pictures lay heavy in memory, and the world had assumed new aspects.

Meanwhile there was ill-health to contend with and war duties to return to.

CHAPTER II

FIRST EXPEDITIONS—SMYRNA

In May of 1948 I had a date with my cousin, Cecil La Fontaine. The meeting-place was to be Bournabat. He was coming down on leave from our Embassy in Ankara and I was arriving from Istanbul.

More than two decades separated us in age, but no one could have been a more welcome companion. Cecil's background of birth and early environment in Bournabat, and his devotion to the world of flowers and mountains, had stamped him in my mind as someone a little apart from other men. Although his Sunday expeditions in Ankara were a feature of Embassy life there, it was the mountains of Smyrna which were his real world—the hills of his youth. So we had the advantage of sensing a link of common feeling between us.

By 1948, after seven years on a strict diet and three serious attacks of jaundice, I was emerging slowly from a twilight of health into the stronger light of more normal living. But I was still not completely robust. Endless walks over the Princes' Islands, where the constant endeavour was learning to get uphill with a minimum of effort, had already given me rhythm of movement and balance, but what seemed missing was stamina.

During our first days in Bournabat we went out on gentle but increasingly long excursions, enjoying the gifts of freedom and sunshine, and the warmth that poured down from the

The Nimph Dağ from the Kiosk : Evening

sky on to the hills. We smelt the good herbs below our feet, and our eyes were delighted by the flowers. Towards evening, when the declining light gleamed over the smooth tract of the Gulf of Smyrna, and the Two Brothers displayed their symmetry as a blue silhouette guarding the waters below, we would return to Bournabat.

Cecil proposed as our first expedition a walk starting at the north-eastern or Nimphio approach to the Nimph Dağ, and ending wherever my strength would allow. We hoped in any case to get to a spring called the Kodjà Su, about a third of the way to the Nimph Dağ summit—possibly even to see the famous Apanocastro or "High Castle," which I had heard a great deal about through the years.

We arranged to meet at 8 A.M. on the Bozalan Square in Bournabat, in front of the house where my Grannie Blanche had lived out her earthly days. It was a quiet morning with the cypresses murmuring softly in the breeze, and a drowsy pall of clouds covering the sky.

We had secured the services of Emin, a cross-eyed chauffeur with a Dodge of antique vintage, whom Cecil held in particular affection, and were soon bumping eastwards across the Smyrna Plain towards the village of Nimphio, which lies beneath the eastern buttresses of the Nimph Dağ.

The village has exceptional charm. Its houses nestle under a host of great plane trees, and the square and its three coffee-houses are completely covered overhead by their thick foliage. It is wonderfully cool and umbrageous, and along the little lanes, fresh, clear water comes flowing down, usually by a channel in the middle of the street. Nimphio has the peace of seclusion ; you hear little but the sound of running waters and the rustle of the leaves above.

Emin's chariot brought us bumping to a halt in the highest part of the village about an hour after we had left Bournabat. In front of us, high on a crag, lay the ruins of the old Lydian castle ; and behind that the massive rocks and ridges, the deep ravines and complicated substructure of the lower Nimph Daǧ.

We swung on our rucksacks with light hearts and left the coffee-houses of Nimphio and the murmuring plane trees, to follow the course of a stream to its secret sources above. Meanwhile the weather had begun to change. There was movement in the clouds, and a veiled but stormy look about the atmosphere.

After we had been going an hour and a half we came to a corner and saw ahead of us a crag crowned with a glory of hanging ivy and sweet alyssum, and cascades of aubrietia. From the bowels of the crag there flowed a tremendous volume of icy water. It was the Kodjà Su. Here we rested and refreshed ourselves with oranges frozen in the water, until after a quarter of an hour I was feeling full of energy again and ready for another stage of the walk.

So we went on towards a commanding crest which looked to the south. Cecil murmured the word "Apanocastro," and I felt a keen anticipation : from the ridge we should see this place which had exercised a kind of spell over me for more than a decade, and which belonged to the very wildest part of the Nimph Daǧ.

It was a long climb to the ridge. Before we got there I noticed far away the slight but unmistakably tempestuous movement of pine branches against the skyline. Presently we heard the sound of wind. Clouds were swinging over fast and the sky was darkening.

A hard gust greeted us at the top. We looked down on the other side. In front of us rose the Apanocastro, like a huge natural fortress with crenellated battlements and rocky towers. Its sides rose perhaps a thousand feet, with savage steepness. Cecil looked at me with a questioning tilt to his eyebrows, a little nervous lest the walk had been too strenuous. I answered the unspoken question, and he chuckled, " Good man. I knew you'd never be able to resist it ! "

We descended a precipitous slope through the pines and crossed a narrow saddle, to find ourselves on the west side of the Apanocastro, where the only practicable route appeared to lie.

The wind had dropped and the woods were silent.

Our way now led up through a maze of rocks and precariously hanging pine trees. We could not see where we were making for, or how close we were to the top. At length, after about fifty minutes, we saw some crags ahead, and above them, not more trees but sky.

Growls of thunder greeted our arrival at the crest. It was a forbidding scene. The upper ridges of the Nimph Dağ were lost in a turmoil of dense vapours. Around us the rocks glittered in a menacing, tawny light.

Suddenly there was a flash which seemed to engulf us, and the air was rent with a shattering explosion. I crouched with my hands over my head and even Cecil seemed daunted. The open, grassy plateau rimmed by crags which forms the summit of the Apanocastro was no place for us on so baleful an afternoon. We started the descent immediately.

It was harder going down than ascending. Several times we had to beat back and change our route. But finally we stood on the saddle again, and the ridge from which we had first looked at the Apanocastro was above us. A few drops of rain came pattering through the pines as Cecil climbed swiftly to the ridge and I followed lagging behind him. Soon we had rejoined our path of the morning. Storms seemed to be assailing all the peaks in the neighbourhood, but we were still miraculously dry, and hurried on down, past Caucasian daisies and tulips, past the Kodjà Su and the aubrietia, and ever on swiftly downwards in the direction of Nimphio.

We were already rounding one of the lower spurs and I could see the castle below us, when Cecil remarked on the whiteness of the fields at the foot of the Manisa Mountains on the other side of the plain. " There must be a lot of daisies," was his theory. But as we looked the daisies gradually extended in area, following the path of a heavy downpour. Then we realised it must be hail. After a minute or two it was clear that the storm was moving across the plain towards us. Shelter must be sought and there was little time to waste.

We were fortunate enough to see a hut near a high cherry orchard, and made for it immediately. A village craftsman was plastering the inside walls ; the owner of the hut, his little son, and a half-wit mute were helping. They bade us a cheerful welcome and we all crouched down inside.

Quite suddenly the storm descended on the hillside. It had become very dark already ; great forks of lightning were shooting every now and then from the clouds to the plain, accompanied by sullen bangs of thunder. Then a gust of wind came up at us, and it began. The hail clattered down on to the roof like a shower of stones. Individual lumps of hail bounced off the ground outside and came

16

ricochetting in through the door. Some were nearly half an inch in diameter. In ten minutes the ground was white.

Half an hour later, after the storm had passed, we thanked our hosts, gave them all our spare food, and walked out down to the path for Nimphio. The air was very cold. Clouds were pouring over the higher ridges, but the lower crags and gorges sparkled brightly in sharp greens and greys. A fresh earthy fragrance came to our nostrils. The leaves dripped ; the hailstones lay in drifts.

In Nimphio the plane trees still watched over the coffee-houses of the square. A few people who were out gazed curiously at us as we passed. Emin greeted us with a mixture of relief and good-humoured indulgence. I have no doubt he thought we were suffering from some form of mental alienation.

By eight o'clock we were back in Bournabat again. After a hot bath I sank into bed, with limbs just congealing into stiffness, but feeling that this first mountain day could scarcely have contained a better mixture of beauty and excitement and good companionship.

II

It was piercingly cold in Bournabat the next day. During the night a north-westerly gale had brought snow right down to two thousand feet, and the hills stood forth in shining white. Cecil spent the day playing the piano and practising music with his friend Richard Abbott. I lounged in the Balliani's sitting-room and reflected that of all the houses I had ever been to none conferred such a feeling of welcome and intimacy as this one.

Before attempting the actual ascent of the Nimph Dağ,

Hidden Valley : the Mahmout Dağ

which was the ambition of my holiday, Cecil had in mind to make an expedition to the Dragon Mountain or Mahmout Dağ, whose bald peak one could see from the hills above Bournabat.

We set off one morning at 7 A.M. under threatening skies, with clouds pressing sombrely on all the mountains. The faithful Emin guided his chariot for us through the small lanes past Nimphio, until forty minutes later we reached the village of upper Kizildja, at the foot of the Mahmout Dağ. The mountain was swathed in mist, but through the clouds we could see the glint of snow.

We started walking at 8.30, and made towards the trail which, once begun, winds up with unbroken steepness to the shoulder before the peak. It was dark and cool, and the forest made it darker. Now and then we had glimpses of towering rocks above. We mounted at a slow, rhythmical pace, without a rest and scarcely a spoken word, right up to the highest spring at three thousand two hundred feet. The dark vault of trees hemmed us in, and underfoot our steps fell silently on to the spongy ground smelling of dank leaf-mould and pine-needles. It was almost like walking in a void. The pleasure lay in the sense of one's surroundings, and in the rhythm maintained through every opposition of surface and gradient. We used so little energy and moved so smoothly that we barely felt warm when we reached the spring.

The ceiling was now only just above us, and a thin rain was falling. Up to the spring the forest had been magnificently thick, with pine trees of majestic stature and arbutus plants growing in profusion. But no sooner had we started onwards than we reached scenes of terrible destruction. A veritable sylvan massacre had taken place. Trunks had been snapped off half-way up and trees lay shattered on the ground. About a fifth of the forest was destroyed. At times the snow and the broken trees held us up and blocked the path. Cecil was dumbfounded ; he had never seen such a thing before. We learnt later in Kizildja that a combination of gale and snow had been responsible.

We came eventually to the bare shoulder above the spring, which was the first level ground in thousands of feet. As a viewpoint it commanded many valleys. To the south we looked down on to the fields of the Mæander Plain far below ; to the west the Nimph Dağ reared up behind the battlements of the Apanocastro.

The top was still wreathed in mist as we stood on the bare grasses of the shoulder, but we decided to go on, and turned leftwards to ascend the peak by the easier eastern approach. Then the clouds began to thin out and we saw, suddenly revealed, a patch of blue sky above us, and snow blazing against it in strident whiteness. Cecil murmured his approval, and we both speeded up. The final rocks were just ahead, and we scrambled up past the last stunted pines on the mountain.

The peak of the Mahmout Dağ is very fine ; a real ridge with drops on both sides, giving a sense of commanding isolation.

We stayed on the top for an hour to eat our lunch and gaze round us. It was cold, and misty in patches. The clouds had not been completely dissipated. Small cotton-wool wisps of vapour came floating along, sometimes below and sometimes above us, rather like what you see from an aeroplane.

We felt exhilarated and yet at rest. A peaceful harmony

had enveloped our universe. The discords and strains of the world were no longer a part of consciousness, but seemed to belong, impersonally, as it were, to another planet. With the fatigue of body the mind was unusually active ; its purview reached out to cover extensions of thought and feeling not normally accessible to men breathing the thicker air of the plains.

We made the descent by a different route through a most beautiful valley. The summit rocks gave way to sparse pines, and then to thicker pines ; finally to the full and majestic trees we had seen on our way up to the spring.

We had even found a species of path and were making good pace when Cecil's eagle eye chanced to alight on a small, half-hidden valley to the east. It was a recondite, sheltered spot, exposed all day to the sun, and it looked very fresh and green at the bottom. " Just the place for peonies ; they might even be out," remarked Cecil. I started to reply, " Just the place for a Snark," but my attempt at humour was left unfinished, for my companion was already charging down a steep declivity under the pines, and he let out a peal of triumph when he reached the bottom. They were indeed peonies. The first I had ever seen in the mountains. And the setting could not have been more attractive. The buds were just opening, and the tender red-pink of the flowers, four or five inches across, contrasted with the burnished green of the foliage. The air was still. The sun shone warmly, bringing to the valley the tints of evening. By the stream the turf was thick and springy. The peonies filled the place with splashes of colour as far as the eye could see.

We stayed for half an hour. It was hard indeed to leave such a spot, but the day was already waning, and we saddled

up our packs with contentment at the unexpected and gracious interlude. As the hidden Peony Valley receded behind us we looked back and saw the flowers still glowing like rubies in the golden light, until they merged slowly into the green of the foliage.

After rejoining our track we came to the finest part of the descent, where the route winds down in craggy steps at the base of an overhang of rock. The path was powder-dry, unreachable by rain; strange pallid plants grew out of crevices, as if furtively seeking the light, but lacking the courage of their convictions.

From the overhang we descended once more into the thickest forest, and eventually, as the shades of evening were lengthening, we came to a place where our track joined the morning's path; below us through the trees we could see the houses of upper Kizildja, and the cypresses, and the minaret. It was the end of the day.

III

Our Smyrna holiday was drawing to its close. From the Balliani's sitting-room I would sit watching the warm evenings merge into night; behind the Two Brothers the light would fade from orange to pale green, and the storks in the garden would clack their bills from the cypresses. The tinkle of water overflowing from the open-air cistern would mingle with the crackle of pine-cones lighting in the bathroom geyser, and whiffs of perfume would drift in from the orange trees; then Aunt Ivy would call us in for dinner. Those were among the best evenings I remember.

" We came to the ridge through eddying mists and puffs of wind. . . ."

(See page 23—Nimph Dağ)

Cecil had left the Nimph Dağ to the end, not only because it would represent the longest excursion, but because I wanted to savour this final achievement last ; an earlier attempt to climb it three years previously had ended in exhaustion half-way up, and an ignominious return. I was twenty-six years old at the time of this holiday in Smyrna with Cecil, and two decades had passed since the childhood visits to Bournabat had first laid before me the vision of its dominance. A certain phase of life seemed to end and a new one to begin, when the Nimph Dağ changed from an unattainable aspiration to a place of knowledge.

Even to-day, after visiting that rocky summit on many occasions, I always feel a tingle of excitement to see it again as the ship noses its way into the Gulf of Smyrna, and the massive pile of the mountain rises above Mount Pagus and the ramparts of the old town. For the Nimph Dağ has a certain magic in its valleys, an elusiveness of beauty, which I have never quite experienced anywhere else. Perhaps the remembered emotion of others and the happiness of ancestors invest certain places with a residuum of good feeling which can never be dispelled.

I thought those days of my forebear who kept his bulb gardens high on the mountain and spent his life in growing flowers ; of the little trains of donkeys descending the Nimph Dağ in the heat of summer, bearing snow for the sick in Bournabat ; and of all the many couples and parties who found joy there in bygone years before a modern materialism had turned people away from most of the pleasures that were not frenzied or gregarious.

With these thoughts in mind I walked along the lane from the Balliani's to the Bozalan Square, which was our meeting-place for 6.45 A.M. on the morning of the Nimph Dağ.

Cecil was there waiting. And the Anglican padré and his wife, who were to accompany us. Emin drove us to Chinar, a village rather smaller and more primitive than Nimphio, at the entrance of a valley before the Nimphio Gorge. Cecil wanted to make the ascent by this approach, and then descend on the Bournabat side to the village of Kavaklidéré.

The ravine leading up from Chinar is very fine ; it is overlooked on the right-hand side by a tall crag called the Soğanasi Rock, past which the path winds up to an alp named Schlosser's Garden.

We reached the Garden in a couple of hours, and saw stretched out in front of us an open expanse of grass, richly green and covered with wild tulips. Rills wandered lazily among the flowers and grasses. Above us towered the summit ridge of the Nimph Dağ, a bare crown of rocks some two thousand feet higher.

After a leisurely halt we started up through the forests between Schlosser's Garden and the rocks, and finally we came to the ridge through eddying mists and puffs of wind. Once on top we could see around, but below us the clouds swirled. The ridge was a desert of limestone blocks, naked, lifeless, and arid. Our position felt very high and remote. We started walking up the ridge westwards. The ground was broken and rocky. Occasionally we met deep hollows like craters, with floors of green grass. Then I saw the summit through the mists, and the triangulation point itself seemingly in movement through the advancing vapours.

Hitherto I had been in good form, with the human machine working smoothly, but the last twenty minutes brought a decline. Heart and lungs began to strain. The others drew ahead and I followed slowly, fighting for breath. The wind tore through my clothes. Then suddenly the slope gave way and I saw the others by the triangulation post. The immense excitement of reaching the summit of the Nimph Dağ gave way to a withdrawal of self and a sense of identification with the cold and the mountain. Cecil greeted me with a smile. "Well, your heart's desire." "Yes," I replied, "at last."

We were standing on the top of the Nimph Dağ. It was half-past twelve and the clouds were driving past.

A momentary clearing gave me the opportunity to take out my binoculars. Yes, there was Bournabat, far below us, miles away: the old cypresses, the Balliani's house, the Kiosk itself, whence so often I had gazed up to this peak where now we stood.

It was too bitter in the wind to linger; Cecil decided we had best descend eight hundred feet and eat our lunch in the sheltered neighbourhood of the Top Spring. We had a comfortable lunch there, out of the wind, away from the clouds, and with a view in front of us through the trees. I found myself too tired, or perhaps too excited, to eat much, and lay listening to the thunder of the wind worrying the ridge above us.

Gradually it became darker. Clouds started swirling down through the trees. We decided to leave the track and go straight on down towards the Kavaklidéré Peony Valley. The ground was overgrown and confused, the slope steep. The padré's wife began to stumble, and the energy

24

with which she had started the day was gone. At length we came to the floor of the Peony Valley. The sky had retired under a burden of gloomy vapours. Below the thick pine branches we walked in a strange, tawny-coloured dimness. Lightning flashed on and off. A few big drops of rain started to clatter down, then stopped.

The upper ridges were now wrapped in storm-clouds and rolls of thunder began reverberating down to us. The atmosphere became ruffled and uneven. Little puffs of breeze played fitfully through the pines. Occasionally we heard a roar of wind buffeting the trees higher up.

I felt the impact of a drop of rain on my shoulder. It was such a big drop that the weight of it was noticeable. Then another came. And another. Suddenly we were conscious of the rain falling everywhere, and the whole forest filled with the rustle of drops. Each drop fell with a kind of a hiss. Each one individually. Every droplet with a personality of its own.

Two minutes later it was coming down with cataclysmic force. The hillsides and gullies dissolved into rushing torrents of red liquid. The path disappeared. A solid wall of dropping water and noise immured us from every sensation but consciousness of the man ahead and the wetness of clothes and shoes. It was useless to think of shelter. We walked squelching on, following Cecil's determined lead, cold and soaked to the skin.

The centre of the storm came up behind us. We had reached the edge of the Kavaklidéré Gorge when the lightning began to strike within a hundred yards of the path. The thunder was terrifying—a sound so violent that it almost knocked one over. We had five flashes practically on top of us. Each time we covered our heads with our hands and were surprised to find ourselves alive at the end of it.

But the centre passed on. After the twenty-minute cloud-burst the rain abated to a steady flow. We clattered along the rocks by the edge of the Kavaklidéré Gorge under lightening skies. Cecil and I were racing ahead. I found the excitement of our experiences had been such as to banish all feeling of tiredness. The noble padré, whose equanimity had never once deserted him throughout the day, was helping along his tired wife with the utmost good humour. And Cecil still clutched a bunch of orchids he had gathered in the Peony Valley.

When we came to cross the stream before the final opening of the vale of Kavaklidéré, we found it had changed from the gentle trickle that Cecil was expecting in the morning to a raging torrent of red water. It was impossible to be wetter than we were, and we crossed it carelessly at the widest point.

The broad level road into the village awaited us. Our day was nearly over and we walked along four abreast. Cecil watched my gait appraisingly, then remarked, " Well, that's what I like to see." The compliment meant a great deal. A year previously it would have been quite impossible for me to cope with such a day. And even as I walked back into Kavaklidéré the vision of the greater hills of the Alps began to beckon as a possibility, where before they had seemed only an ideal.

CHAPTER III

THE BITHYNIAN OLYMPUS

In the days of my childhood I did not look towards greater things than the Blue Mountains, which stood out so plainly across the Sea of Marmora from our house. As the years went by, however, I began to pay more and more attention to the remoter and higher line of the Bithynian Olympus, or Uludağ of modern Turkish geography, whose snows glinted in the sky behind the Princes' Islands on clear days. The mountain lies behind the town of Bursa, about seventy miles from Istanbul as the crow flies, which is a fair distance for the unaided human eye to encompass at sea level.

During my summer holidays from school in England I made quite a collection of Uludağ photos taken from our attic and using a Zeiss 6× binocular as a telephoto lens. This brought the range relatively close, but it always remained something of a remote elysium in those days. My parents had no sympathy for mountain aspirations and were strongly opposed to any such enthusiasm.

A whole decade was to roll by before I started making my way to Bursa and planning trips up the Uludağ. Bursa lies on the very flank of the mountain and perhaps has more beauty than any exclusively Turkish town in the country. An orientalist of some repute once told me that he considered there were only two supremely lovely towns in the Middle

East—Isfahan and Bursa—and that he would be hard put to choose which was first. There is no doubt that the view from the minaret of the Green Mosque in Bursa towards the Mosque of Emir Sultan, standing so nobly on its hill against the mountain backdrop, must be one of the finest urban views in the world.

The Turkish houses, mostly of village style, are gaily coloured but blend with the landscape. Below the houses lies the verdant plain. Above them, the foothills of the Bithynian Olympus. Long before Constantinople was captured by the Conqueror in 1453, Bursa was serving as the first capital of the Ottoman Empire, and the story of its siege is to Turkish history almost what the siege of Troy is to Hellenistic. It is said that Sultan Yavuz Selim directed one of the assaults from the summit of an isolated buttress of the mountain which still bears his name to-day. The valiant Sultan must have been possessed of better than usual eyesight, for this summit is five thousand feet above the plain and several miles from the town.

The history of Bursa goes back to long before the Osmanlis, for the town had already acquired importance in Roman days. The Bithynian Olympus was venerated at that time as a holy mountain ; even to-day traces of original Roman flagstones can be found high up in steep places. The so-called Kilissé Dere, or "Valley of the Churches," contains numerous monastic remains dating back to the earliest part of the first millennium A.D., when it was a favourite place of retirement for Christian saints and hermits. The Turks called the mountain " Keshish Daǧ," or " Mountain of Monks," and this name persisted through the centuries until very recent times.

During the past five years I have made a great number

In a Bournabat garden

of trips to Bursa and the Uludağ—perhaps twenty-five or
twenty-six—and there must be few visitors, if any, with the
same knowledge of the mountain. Under the impact of
repetition the pictures have inevitably become blurred, but
many fair memories still remain to brighten the evenings of
winter. One of the best of these goes back to the year of
the Nimph Dağ and the Apanocastro, when I visited the
Uludağ in October and made my first stay on high places
in the good company of David, Philippa, and Yolande.

II

We had taken the ferry-boat to Yalova on the opposite
coast of the Marmora, and boarded from there an ancient
bus which was to carry us the fifty-odd miles to Bursa. The
driver was a fierce-looking, mustachioed individual, who wore
an incongruous white peaked cap. He rejoiced in the name of
"Pireli Mehmet," meaning "Flea-ridden Mehmet," and drove
with great verve and audacity. There are two watersheds to
cross on the road and the drive is full of interest. I remember
flea-ridden Mehmet racing neck and neck with another bus
down a fearsome descent. We had a full complement of
passengers, some minor livestock inside, as well as two rams
lashed down with the luggage on to the roof. All of which
were delivered safely in Bursa, including the long-suffering
rams. Shortly after this journey I regret to record that
flea-ridden Mehmet fell on the field of honour, a casualty
to his own daring, when the bus he was driving went over
the edge, and, to use the words of the Turkish newspaper
report, " Became small pieces."

The car that was waiting for us in Bursa that afternoon bore us up through the early scrub and chestnut belt of the mountain, past the autumn shades of the deciduous forests, and into the sombre aisles of the pines and the spruce trees.

Finally we rounded a corner to the south, and the cold, naked slopes of the summit ridge—Zirvé cliffs, the last col, and Zirvé Peak—swung into view, pale-lit in the evening light, but remote and withdrawn, strangely aloof and grey. Ahead lay the Refuge, where we would sleep in the nights to come. We paid off the car and left the world behind us.

Apart from the caretaker we were the only people on the mountain ; in the Refuge there reigned a bitter cold. Through its double windows we looked northwards across the long plateau of the upper Uludağ, which effectively cut us off from the plain and from all sight of the haunts of men. There was nothing but the air and the spruces, and the sound of a wind in the trees.

We had taken one and a half hours to come up in the car. The Refuge was in shadow and the sun about to set. I proposed a quick climb to Cennet Kaya, the Paradise Rock. We put on our warmest clothes and went out.

The clink and grit of nails on firm rock was music to the ear. To breathe the cold invigorating atmosphere and use effort in the thinner air brought an extra rush of healthy blood coursing through the body. I felt the rapturous sense of energy and muscular co-ordination. Philippa announced that the effects of three days' illness had suddenly left her. We scrambled up to the crest behind the Refuge over slabs of granite set with juniper shrubs and grass ; then climbed to the highest point of Paradise Rock, some seventy feet

30

above the ridge, just as the sun was setting in a sea of flaming cloud.

Its slightly flattened globe began to sink behind a range in the far west. The range was intensely blue. On its crest we could just discern the indented suggestion of trees. The last glimmer of the sun disappeared, and there was nothing left but air and wind and flaming cloud ; blue ridges and grey ridges and the solitude of heights.

As an introduction to the upper world this was a moment of revelation made perfect by the sense of feeling shared between us all, and by reticence. We sat for many minutes in silence, and then walked down to the Refuge, where a hot stove and supper awaited us.

From my high bunk that night I could see through the dormer window on to the vague lines of the forest. The air in the spruces sighed with the cold, remote sound of wind in the mountains. I felt the increased beat and flow of blood in the veins, the slightly quicker respiration, and also a sense of alertness and life unknown to me before. The thought of the expeditions ahead in the next three days, of all the delicious uncertainty of places and routes and new beauties to see, lay before me, extended into the future like a dream, but a dream capable of realisation. It was on this night that I had for the first time the real feeling of the mountains, the sweep of limitless horizons and the sense of fulfilment in high places—separate from all childhood associations.

Next morning the sun was warming with colour the slopes below the Refuge as we looked on to them from our bunks. But the grasses and leaves outside were rimmed with ice crystals. The mountain was radiant and inviolate, asking to be explored. Inside us all a surging energy responded.

31

We went into the luminous, crystal air and took the path northwards along a spur of the plateau towards the crag of Bakadjik, with its extraordinary aerial view of the mosques of Bursa five thousand feet beneath. Thence we walked under the velvety shade of the spruce forest towards the pools of Softaboğan. Above us, to the south, rose the gaunt rocks of Zirvé Peak, enfolding pockets of aged snow. They were well above the tree-line, those rocks, and I had the sense of being at last among the upper peaks where always I had longed to be.

III

The Uludağ enfolds widely different types of scenery, and one can experience almost every kind of mountain pleasure there. Above the forest of spruce and beech, and the rounded rocks of the Granite Zone, comes the ultimate bareness of the summit ridge—a waste of limestone and marble slabs, some ten miles long. The ridge breaks down to the north in cliffs; at their base lie old névé snow-drifts, and lakes, nine in number, hemmed in by ancient moraine beds. It is under these cliffs, especially when the snow is melting, that one has a feeling of almost alpine severity in the surroundings.

Perhaps the finest walk below the tree-line is the Orman Yolu, or " Forest Way," on the south side of the mountain. And its best moment comes when the path makes a sudden turn and reveals the immense craggy cirque of the Marble Mountain, whose rocks soar up one thousand six hundred feet from their base in the beech forest. Near the foot of the rocks, in the centre of the great amphitheatre, there is a spring shaded by massive beeches.

32

The view from Bakadjik—Uludağ

It is at this spring that I have whiled away many a warm afternoon in summer, surrounded by the most impressive scenery that the Uludağ can provide. The place is a favourite with shepherds, who drive up their flocks from the village of Soğukpinar in the valley to small corrals in the neighbourhood of the spring. A flock of sheep is often a danger to travellers in Anatolia, owing to the accompanying dogs. These huge and ferocious beasts stand as much as three feet high and have collars with iron spikes round their necks for protection against the wolves. But a word from the shepherd will usually silence them.

Several times near the spring I have approached quietly and heard the sound of the shepherd boy's pipe played with lamenting Eastern rhythm, but somehow in keeping with its setting. Usually they stop when they see a stranger, but once not long ago we persuaded a shepherd boy to go on playing for us, and lay all of an early autumn afternoon stretched out beside the beeches, listening to the sound of the mountain stream mingle with the rustle of leaves and the strains of the pipe. The afternoon was warm, with more than a hint of sultriness. In the ambit of rock walls above us the clouds were beginning to form and melt, to chase round and boil and turn, as though they were brewing in some gigantic cauldron. Rarely on the mountains does the temperature make us completely at ease; often it is too cold and sometimes too hot, but on this afternoon we had the excellent mean, and lay like the gods in Tennyson's 'Lotos-eaters,' careless of mankind.

When I asked him about his dogs, the shepherd boy was glad to talk. He said they were crossed with wolves to make them hardier and more savage. The only enemy he knew

c

33

on the hills was the wolf pack, but with good dogs he seldom suffered any losses. In his grandfather's day they owned a wonderful dog who could be trusted to guard a certain col and keep the wolves out (there was no other way for them to approach), so that they had peace and security within the fold throughout many years. When this dog died they trained the finest of their remaining dogs to carry on the tradition. For some months the successor guarded the col faithfully. Then one night a whole pack of wolves came in, accompanied by the sheep-dog, which had turned traitor. A terrible slaughter ensued among the sheep; and on the following day the other dogs tore the traitor to pieces. From then onwards they never put a single dog into such a position of trust.

The story seems quaint, if charming, down at sea level, but on that afternoon we considered it gravely. It was all part of the mountain scene.

Towards evening the freshening air melted away the clouds, and we started walking delicately up the poised blocks of the scree slope towards the face of the Marble Mountain. The route led through a maze of gullies and pinnacles, with views of exhilarating steepness below us. The short footstep, the grateful handhold, an occasional tight rope for number three, and wherever possible, rhythm of movement, were the things I tried to show and provide for my companions; so that when the last minutes of day arrived two hours later, it was a fresh and unjaded party that assembled on the peak of the Marble Mountain.

Down by the Orman Yolu path below us, the setting sun was firing the autumn forests of the lower slopes. Their colouring was of extraordinary brilliance, and glowed as if lighted from within by some mysterious incandescence. On the uppermost slope leading to Zirvé, with its eight-thousand-foot summit poised high against the sky, the light was soft and vibrant in quality, so rich in tone that the marble slopes seemed to pulse in it.

Standing up we watched the day fade and the sun die, till the shiver of twilight seized us. The air seemed to contract. The cold of the upper atmosphere descended. As we watched, luminous, ray-like forms flooded up into the heavens from the antipodes of the sunset. Their faint brightness, through which the stars filtered, was the last effulgence of day, and brought before the imagination the distances of interstellar space, empty, inconceivably empty, and cold.

We raced down the juniper slopes on the north side of the Marble Mountain to reach the road while there was still a trace of daylight, then walked back to the Refuge under the light of the constellations, through the frigid motionless air, past the silhouettes of the spruces. The crests of the ridge seemed black and mysterious; the Refuge showed dim-lighted windows through the trees, and the Wincharger creaked softly.

IV

For the moderately active visitor to the mountain there are few more wonderful things than the wealth of flowers in summer. The best time is early June, when the snows have retreated to the higher slopes and when water is running on all sides. I have found *Gentiana asclepiadea*, with magnificent scent and profusion of flower, growing thirty inches

35

high near the spring below the Marble Mountain. Within ten yards of these giant gentians could be seen quantities of geums and tall primulas.

The lakes are another place where primulas and geums grow mixed. The contrast here between the alpine severity of the rock and moraine scenery and the tender green grass and orange and mauve flowers is one of the most striking to be seen on the Uludağ.

The whole of the summit ridge is studded with brilliant blue gentians and clumps of *Eritrichium nanum*. These two flowers are perhaps the most glorious of all the alpine fraternity, and their colouring is nowhere seen to better advantage than against the grey-white slabs and pink androsace and stonecrop with which they are mingled on the upper Uludağ.

Flowers are one of the most precious gifts of the hills. And their steadfast growing and yearly fading, and their eternal renewal and period of glory, renew us to ourselves ; so that we find always the same delight in the unchanging assurance of their victory over the snows and cold of winter.

Summer on the Uludağ is also the season of the snow-cutters. And if there is any sound which has for me a magic quality on the mountain, it is the distant tinkle of bells in the night, sounding far down in the forest below the Refuge. As the bells come nearer, the watcher will see, if he goes to a window, a line of donkeys and mules coming slowly up the road. A faint dust rises from their hooves and shows up in the scintillant light of the moon. The spruces line the way like frozen statues, and their shadows lie blue on the granity path. Now the caravan is passing the Refuge. The bells sound strongly as the two drivers on the leading mules

36

ride past. Behind them the tethered donkeys follow. And now the tinkle of bells lessens, until once again it falls faintly on the ear and finally vanishes into the night.

The snow-cutters ride on for another hour, then mount the screes to the snow-pit in the hollow under Zirvé cliffs. There they unstring their axes and start their labour. Cubes of hard névé snow are cut and stored in panniers lined with felt and covered with spruce boughs. Each animal is loaded with a pannier on both sides, and before the eastern skies have reddened with dawn the caravan is once again in movement on the journey seven thousand feet downwards to Bursa. The snow-cutters leave the frozen silence of the snow-pit, and within five hours they are sweating in the 90° shade heat of the town. It must be a hard life, demanding fortitude and immense stamina, both of which the Anatolian peasant possesses in abundance. The snow is sold in Bursa for the equivalent of perhaps a penny a pound, and enters the ice-boxes of the town to cool the butter and fruit of the population.

The profession of snow-cutter is an ancient and even honoured calling. It is also the appanage of a few families only. I am told that the snow-cutters in some cases still possess " Firmans," or royal letters of appointment from the Sultanate, dating back as far as the reign of Suleiman the Magnificent. The profession of snow-cutting in Bursa was for centuries restricted by edict to these families, and passed down from father to son.

Even in ancient times the Sultan's snow was quarried from the same snow-pit as the cutters use to-day, and probably carried on the backs of the ancestors of the same donkeys. Once in Bursa a special runner service of fleet horses bore

37

Softaboğan Pool—Uludağ

the snow to the port of Mudanya. And from Mudanya fast sailing vessels, whom no one had the power to delay under pain of the imperial displeasure, carried the precious and perishable cargo to the walls of the Seraglio at Constantinople. It is curious to reflect that the sherbets which the Sultan employed to slake his imperial thirst were cooled with snow from the Bithynian Olympus that had probably taken three days to accomplish its journey.

v

One of my best memories of the Uludağ was a two-night trip made with Perry Hart and Henning Simonsen. The company of outstanding talent, perhaps genius, is any case a privilege, and Perry's unusual awareness and response to the mountain moods of the day will stand out for always in my mind. As for Henning, gaiety and humour streamed from him like light from the sun. I think we were almost more aching in our muscles from laughter on this trip than from the heaviness of our rucksacks. There was no mean weight in the latter, for we came up in a highly independent frame of mind, armed with bivouac equipment and resolved to avoid the summer crowds at the Refuge.

We spent our first night under the spruces near Paradise Rock, feeling very snug in down sleeping-bags. The next day I showed Perry and Henning the Orman Yolu and the Marble Mountain ambit. We ascended the south face by an easy route, and Henning kept us in constant laughter at his buffoonery over a large black umbrella he had thoughtfully provided himself with as a protection for his Danish skin

38

from the baleful sun of Turkey. We raced down the Marble Mountain peak to the pool of Softabogan for a bathe, and thence up to Bakadjik Point, all in one perfect day of mountain action.

Bakadjik Point saw a weary but happy party cooking an early dinner. By eight o'clock we were warm in our bags, Perry in the middle, and Henning and I on the outsides. I had seen some bear tracks on the path nearby and we teased Perry unmercifully about the bears. Henning told her she would wake up in the night, feeling a hand on her shoulder and mumble sleepily, " Stop it, Ashenden," only to find the hand was a paw : there would be no Henning and no Ashenden left, but only a great bear with flaming eyes.

It grew bitterly cold. Below us the lights of Bursa twinkled upwards. Above us in the still air the heavens blazed with a thousand points of icy fire. Shooting stars coursed by in greater numbers than I have ever seen before, and a heavy dew fell on our outer covers.

At four o'clock it was only one degree above freezing-point, and we rose shivering, to pack up hurriedly and start the walk down, which was to be the highlight of the trip so far as Henning and Perry were concerned.

By the time we left it was full dawn and the sun was just about to rise. Henning's rucksack looked a most amazing sight, with the black umbrella furled and strapped to the outside base, surmounted by an enormous surface of lightly rolled, damp sleeping-bag. Various bottles and other accoutrements were visible, including a heavy enamel shaving-mug, which swung and clanged at each step. I believe Henning had brought this mug just for my benefit, knowing my fanatical views on weight-saving and economy of effort.

39

As we swung over the brink and down the initial curves of the Bakadjik descent, the sun came up. The first hour of the Bakadjik route is sensational. The path is exceedingly steep, almost too steep to walk on, and the exposure is considerable in places. But everywhere it is safe, as the edges are built up with blocks of stone. Underfoot one treads occasional flagstones which are of Roman origin. The track winds down the wooded and rocky escarpment, traversing granite faces on narrow parapets, plunging into steep forest, and gradually working down to the base of the six-hundred-foot granite obelisk of Bakadjik Rock. Most of the time we had tremendous views downwards into Bursa five thousand feet below. The early light of morning had caught the domes and minarets of the town, and picked out every detail of architecture and lie of ground. It began to get noticeably less cold. We shed clothes, and our sleeping-bags started to dry.

Presently we reached the lower woodland part of the way and the long descent began through those cool umbrageous paths, damp and hidden, under a ceiling of leaves and walls of branches. We had left the Granite Belt of the mountain and the loose stones of gneiss and schist were a trial on the path. Henning and I were each carrying about thirty-five pounds.

My altimeter crept slowly down. 1400 metres, 1300, 1200, 1100, then a long period of descent when I steadfastly refused to look at it, and . . . 900.

It was getting hot by now. We came down to shirts and trousers. The Bursa Plain when we looked at it appeared quite close, and faint sounds of civilisation began to reach us. A cock crowed thinly from below. And this

40

sound brought home to us that we were returning to the world of ordinary life. The cock was the end of our short mountain idyll.

At last we left the woodland belt and, less than a thousand feet above the plain, came to open stony paths, with evergreen shrubs and bushes on either side, under occasional old chestnut trees. The air was hot and sluggish by now. Somehow lazy and thick. So different to the pure air of the mountains. And the sun shone fiercely.

A train of mules carrying wood to some upper pasture came towards us on the track, and we stopped to let them pass. Henning was some way behind, and we heard a commotion when they got to him. The second mule reared up and broke his tethering rein, so that the whole caravan was thrown into confusion. Apparently the sight of Henning in his extraordinary get-up of umbrella and sleeping-bags, with the shaving-mug clanging, had scared the whole mulish fraternity.

" Wait till you see what the street boys will do to you when we get into Bursa," I said grimly. But Henning was past caring. He and Perry were singing Mozart opera to each other and continued right on into the town. I walked ahead partially disowning them, but feeling the occasion too good for anything less than a rendering of the " An die Freude " theme of the Ninth Symphony.

That same afternoon we gathered in goodly number in the ballroom of Edwin Whittall's residence, to hear Perry perform the Mendelssohn Concerto—with Cecil playing the orchestral accompaniment—as well as the Bach Chaconne and the Wieniawski Légende. The setting of that great room, with the Gobelins tapestries and the deep plush sofas, gave a feeling of eighteenth-century spaciousness. I do not think I have ever been so stirred by music. And as I write these lines Edwin Whittall lies dying, the last of his generation. Before this book is finished the old mansion will be sold, and all the traditions and way of life that went with it will have vanished for always. But at least before the end Perry played for us there, with that deep integrity and musicianship which will soon be filling the concert halls of the world. And when she was asked how *she* thought the Chaconne had gone, the answer was, " Well, technically, maybe I've played it better ; but spiritually, never." Which was perhaps a tribute to the Uludağ.

CHAPTER IV

THE ADVENTURE OF THE UNKNOWN
WATERFALL

I HAD done several expeditions to the Uludağ before I discovered some of the good places on the peninsula of the Argonthonius—or " Blue Mountains " of my childhood. And whereas going to the Uludağ involved securing a couple of days' leave, it was possible to visit the Blue Mountains in an ordinary week-end, which was a distinct advantage.

For some years I had heard vague reports from peasants and villagers of a great waterfall somewhere in the valleys west of Yalova. The region is wild and rather inaccessible ; apart from a littoral of sparse villages fringing the peninsula it is completely mountainous and deserted. Although the crests rise only to three thousand feet, the steepness of their sides and the density of the forest make them difficult of approach.

We had tried no less than three times to attain the waterfall, but had always been compelled by the approach of night to give up without finding it. Once our party had caught a glimpse of what seemed to be a distant ribbon of whiteness tumbling over lofty crags, and the question of where the waterfall actually lay was no longer quite such a problem. It remained only to organise a group of good walkers capable of carrying their own sleeping-bags and equipment for a two-day excursion.

43

We ended up with Edgar Hirzel, an indefatigable Swiss friend; Kotcho Avgustides, a sportsman and shot of some repute; and Yolande Whittall, whose taste for adventurous trips has always been keenly developed.

It was a hot July evening when we left Istanbul by a ferry-boat bound for Yalova port, on the opposite side of the Marmora, about thirty miles away. The ferry service is swift, comfortable, and efficient. We were soon cutting through the blue waters, past the Princes' Islands and out into the open sea, at a steady twelve knots. The islands are now a summer pleasure resort, but fifteen hundred years ago they were the appointed place of exile for the Princes and nobles of Byzantium who happened to fall foul of the Emperor. Like Capri they have a history (although a less sinister one), and as the ferry-boat left I thought to myself that there must have been many fates more unpleasant than to be taken across the waters of the Propontis and left to tend a garden on the island of Prinkipo.

A strong wind from the north tore through the rigging and whipped up the waves. As we reached Yalova the sun was setting, and when we looked up to our ridges of the morrow they were stained a warm mauve ; in between, the valleys were filled with velvety blue shadows, full of mystery. Even after many expeditions, and climbs of greater stature, I felt a pleasant thrill at the thought that perhaps on the next day we might be entering fastnesses never visited till now.

From Yalova port a car bore us up the seven or eight miles of road to Yalova Baths. This is a resort in the hills famous since the days of the Emperor Justinian for its hot mineral waters, and now graced by several hotels. Unfor-

On the Marble Mountain—Uludağ

tunately all these appeared to be full, and after an agreeable dinner at a restaurant under the trees, where the air seemed curiously still and bland after the acrid tang of the waves, we repaired for the night to a village nearby. Here we slept in a house built of mud, with floors of dried earth. A gracious peasant landlady of Circassian origin tended to our wants and bid us an early good-night.

At 3.30 A.M. on the morrow we were due to start in a taxi for the village of Kocadéré, roughly half-way between Yalova and the apex of the peninsula. It was from here that we would begin the walk. Our first objective was a place in the mountains known by the encouraging name of " Dipsiz Göl " or " Bottomless Lake " ; after this we planned to swing round and approach the waterfall from the west, returning to Yalova Baths by a path supposed to follow the main watershed along the tops of the ridges.

Unfortunately our taxi-driver played us false and we only got off at five. The way to Kocadéré must be less than twenty miles, but it took one and a half hours to cover, as the track is little more than vestigial in places. When we arrived there it was already morning, and the early sun had picked out the minaret of the mosque above the plane trees and rooftops of the village.

The local headman seemed suspicious and uneasy. We told him we were bound for the Dipsiz Göl and asked him which way we should go. This elicited the usual replies : (a) The taxi could not take us there (!) ; (b) It was too far to walk ; (c) We should never find it anyway because the paths were too confusing. Eventually, however, a track running through the olive groves was pointed out to us and we left the village to the accompaniment of much head-shaking and

45

general puzzlement as to what might be the true (as opposed to the declared) object of our walk. The size of our rucksacks in particular excited comment, and malicious tongues implied that we might be going to look for treasure. All this is unfortunately too typical of the local mentality, and should have served as a warning of what was to befall us later in the day. At the time, though, we laughed it off.

Edgar had a prismatic compass, while I was armed with a contour map of sorts and my efficient Swiss double-dial altimeter, so we felt sure we would be able to find our way to the lake, notwithstanding the headman's dire prophetics.

We set off under the olive trees and were soon climbing a spur leading up to the mountains in front of us. It was a damp, rather muggy morning, and the upper ridges were swathed in vapour. We climbed steadily through low shrubs and trees. In places the path was cut deep into the hill so that we had to walk single file up a narrow cleft roofed with greenery. A fork confronted us with a choice of routes and we took the left-hand path after a brief look at the " instruments." Edgar and Yolande were alternately setting the pace and we went fast.

After three-quarters of an hour we were about a thousand feet up, and stopped to have a breather. The shrubs had given way to chestnut trees and the woods were getting thicker and finer. We were now on a ridge heading due south towards the main crest, where clouds still pressed sombrely on the peaks.

I had heard that the Dipsiz Göl was "A lake surrounded by pine trees near the top of the mountains." We were all rather sceptical about this because none of us had ever seen a pine tree on the Yalova Peninsula, and so it was with some

46

surprise that, topping a small hill, we saw above us on the skyline a dark indented crest that was unmistakably coniferous. The lake could not be far off now, I thought, and Edgar gave a chuckle at the idea of what the headman had told us. On my map the lake was not actually marked, but the area we were heading for was shown as " Ridges near the Dipsiz Göl." We pressed on.

The path steepened, and we came to the first pine trees growing here and there among the chestnuts, with occasional beeches and silver birch. It was a beautiful spot, and I had seldom seen trees of such variety growing in one place. Every now and then we got glimpses of the emerald waters of the Marmora through the valleys on our right. The clouds on the high ridges seemed quite close by this time, and an agreeable sense of height and isolation began to gain us. As we came up to the indented crest a cool wind from the north started to blow across, and the air seemed already lighter and purer to breathe, with that resinous, slightly acrid fragrance of pines giving a tang to the atmosphere.

We were on a small plateau about eighteen hundred feet above the sea, and just beside us was a hut with a ladder above it, reaching up to a sort of crow's-nest. The occupant told us he was a fire watchman, and pointed rather proudly to a telephone in his hut. " When there is a fire," he said, " I telephone down to the village," and took up the instrument and rang several times, just to show us how. Unfortunately there was nobody at the other end of the line, and our friend smiled ruefully. " When it is like that, one has to use one's legs. Walking is the more sure in the end." He gave us cool water from a pitcher and told us where to find the lake.

I liked the fire watchman. He was a friendly, simple man, who took us for what we were, without suspicion or hostility, and his gentle manner and young, rather melancholy face had imprinted on it the detachment and tranquillity of those who lead lonely lives far from their kind.

After twenty minutes we came to the lake, which is set deep in the woods and fringed by reeds and ferns. There was an outflow trickling away from the east, and the water went down a ravine where the stones glinted a dull, metallic black that made one think of iron.

Overlooking the lake and close to the stream was an open bank. The place invited repose. We took off our packs and lay down, while a few thin rays of sunlight came through the mists above and lit the scene with gentle radiance. Edgar and Yolande went to sleep, and it was not until three-quarters of an hour later that we saddled up again.

The next hour was probably the grandest part of the day's walking. Our way led through majestic beech forests which clothed the mountain-sides in a cool canopy of green that hung far above our heads. A heavy, brooding silence lay everywhere. The way was steep. Sometimes up and sometimes down. It was very dry, and old leaves rustled underfoot. We traversed narrow ravines where no stream flowed, but where the smooth channelling of rocks above us pointed to waterfalls in the wet season. Great lumps of mineral magnetite lay here and there, and the dark, ferruginous glimmer of the gullies made it seem almost like walking in a dream. I have never felt a place so remote and secluded from the world.

Edgar reckoned we must be on the flanks of the Karlik Dağ (Mountain of Snows), and not far from the waterfall

48

itself, which in our previous attempts we had tried to approach from the other side, only to be confronted by " impossible " terrain. My altimeter showed just over two thousand feet when we came round a corner and heard the unmistakable sound of water dropping into depths somewhere far below us. The slope was exceedingly steep, a mixture of earth and rock, with sturdy bushes added as an obstacle, and roofed always with the same majestic beeches, which now swung and rustled in the breeze. I wanted to force the descent at once and attain what seemed undoubtedly our goal ; but other counsels prevailed and we continued along our path, hoping at every step to discover a way down on the left which would get us to the fall with greater ease. And so we went on for some time, while the path steadily mounted, and the slopes down remained uncompromisingly hostile. Finally the track turned leftwards and began to descend, our hopes rising accordingly. But the gradient was too gentle, and soon we had emerged from the forest on to a smooth upland pasture, where the grass grew green and rich and the ground was level. It was clear we had overshot the waterfall.

We decided to work along a shallow valley leading north from the pasture and see if we could join up with the main watercourse and reach our objective before lunch. It was now a quarter to twelve, and we went back into the woods again, almost in the direction we had come from. But the valley was exceedingly dense and confused, with streams running in all directions, seemingly defying the laws of gravity. We were deflected again and again from our true direction by labyrinthine obstacles and deviations. The sun had come out and chased the mists away, so that our efforts became

D

more laborious and the packs grew heavier and heavier. I called a halt for lunch, as we were only wasting our strength, and we lay down by a stream under the trees and started in on the food.

A light sleep followed and it was two o'clock before we began again. Yolande was all for finding our waterfall no matter how long it took, but I had my mind on the time and reckoned we ought to do a good part of our way back to Yalova before the approach of night. After further in-effectual searchings, where our rate of progress must have been less than half a mile an hour—and at great cost in effort—we finally gave up the waterfall, knowing that once more it had beaten us.

We regained the little pasture and swung due south towards the main upper plateau and watershed of the range. In a quarter of an hour we reached wide, open meadows, where huts of lath and a tent met our eyes. There were cattle grazing, and horses. A breeze blew cool and sharp. It was a cheerful spot.

The fire watchman had told us about an old man called Bahri Djan who lived there, and we soon found him and made his acquaintance. After hearing about the fire watch-man, he showed great courtesy and friendliness, but was unable to give us any good news about the way back. It seemed that the track along the crest of the range no longer existed, having been choked up for the last forty years. So much for my map!

It was clear that to reach Yalova we would have our work cut out. All the paths over the Argonthonius evidently led north and south and there was nothing going from east to west. Without some sort of trail the forest was impenetrably thick. Bahri Djan advised us to go over the range and continue on south and east until we came to the village of Kumla, lying not far from Gemlik on the other side of the peninsula. From Kumla we would be able to take the way which the old German Field-Marshal Von der Goltz had made famous in his account of the first crossing of the Argonthonius.

Bahri Djan came with us for three-quarters of an hour, just to set us on the right path and take us over the crest of the range. He was a Turk of the old peasant class, with whom hospitality to strangers and gentlemanly feeling were second nature. We shook hands and said good-bye to him with real regret.

It was now four o'clock and we were on a south slope with the path leading towards where the sea must be, in the opposite direction to where we wanted to go. The forest had thinned to low woods and the sun was warm. I espied a path leading off leftwards to the east, and insisted on taking it in spite of doubts raised by the others. The track turned more and more to the left until we were travelling north-east, exactly where we wanted to go. Edgar had his nose to the compass like a bloodhound, and our hopes began to rise. But the satisfaction was short-lived ; the path swung round farther and farther, and eventually we were pointing back to the waterfall.

After retracing our steps we cut across a belt of forest and came out again to where we judged the other track should be passing. Here the forest ended and a wide plateau opened out to the south. In the middle of it rose a kind of tumulus, with tall trees soaring to the sky. We remembered suddenly that Bahri Djan had told us we had to pass a clump of trees ; this was obviously the place. We mounted the tumulus and were astonished to find oaks. They must have been planted very close together, and grew straight upwards in the struggle for light and air. The evening sunlight fell slantingly past their trunks and lit with gold the ground beneath, while a strong wind roared through the upper foliage, a full seventy or eighty feet above our heads.

From here our way led southwards and eastwards, ever onwards and downwards, in the general direction of Gemlik. And now we had left the woods and were moving through scrub. The day had been a long one, and Yolande and Kotcho were beginning to lag behind. My one thought from this moment on was to find water so that we could stop for the night, and get into our sleeping-bags. We needed water, firstly to drink, and secondly to make our Birchermüsli for breakfast the following morning. We had brought along with us all the ingredients of this celebrated Swiss dish—hazel-nuts, almonds, dried fruit, oatmeal, lemon, tinned milk, and sugar—and Edgar had nobly saddled himself with a monster utensil, fit for feeding half an army, in which it was proposed to concoct the thing.

But water eluded us. All the valleys were dry and the springs waterless. We were forced farther and farther down, until the blue waters of the Gulf of Gemlik broke suddenly into view and the slopes of the Bithynian Olympus rose high into the sky on our right. I wanted to avoid all villages like the plague, and sleep if possible in the woods, but the harsh necessity for water drove us on over crests and ridges, until we came at last to a valley where a stream flowed lazily past grassy banks.

It was after 9 P.M. and the sun had departed. We had been up since before half-past three in the morning, and out on the walk for almost fifteen hours. Edgar's stride had lost little of the vigour and elasticity of the morning, even though he was carrying more than any of us and had taken over Kotcho's gun during the last two hours. My own rucksack had been made heavier by Kotcho's sleeping-bag, which I had appropriated earlier in the day, and we had not had anything to eat for many hours. Meanwhile Yolande had continued to carry her full pack in the most exemplary manner, in spite of suffering from a strained foot (we did not know this until the next day). As for myself, I had never before taken such a weight on a long day and my shoulders were feeling like dropping off; so it was rather a weary party that sank under the lee of a small bank and opened rucksacks for evening supper. Except perhaps for Edgar, I think the day had extended us fully.

A villager from Kumla who passed by in the last crepuscular light seemed rather uneasy at seeing us; he offered to lead us to his village, but we were too tired to want to go there, and said we would spend the night where we were. His surprise and suspicion at this answer was only too obvious, and though we thanked him and said we would visit Kumla on the morrow, he went off in rather an odd manner.

After this we shifted our position to a more sheltered place and rolled out our sleeping-bags for the night under the thin light of the moon. Supper was a heavenly luxury, accompanied by drowsiness, relaxation, and a sense of complete mental and physical well-being; the comforts of food and water bore away the fatigues and strains of the day, until we had sunk into a quiet torpor, ready for the sleep of night. Above us the stars glittered in a pale sky and the half-moon began to wane against the west.

It was at this moment that we saw the ghostly forms of two horsemen coming silently over the grass towards the spot where we had met the villager. They stopped and searched, then looked about them and muttered a few words. But evidently they did not find what they were looking for, and cantered off, baffled, in the direction of Kumla. I had an uneasy feeling that we were the object of the search, but felt too comfortable to worry much.

The sound of summer crickets and the rippling voice of the stream bore us quietly from where we were to the furthest confines of sleep.

The next thing I remember was a hoarse shout, and the sound of men running towards us. Edgar's torch flashed. Then a lantern came from nowhere out of the darkness, and I saw the glitter of rifle barrels. A great dog towered above our sleeping-bags. In a trice we were surrounded. There seemed very little one could do, for twelve men, all armed with rifles, had closed in. My first feeling was one of intense annoyance that we should have had our richly earned slumbers brought so harshly to a halt. But fortunately I kept my mouth shut and said nothing. Edgar rose to the occasion splendidly and greeted our friends in the most casual manner possible, as if he had been used throughout his life to being surrounded by armed desperadoes, at any hour of the night. The men were hostile and suspicious. They questioned us over and over again, and seemed incapable of understanding that we were out for our pleasure. The fact that Kotcho had a shot-gun and that both he and Edgar carried shooting licences was the one thing about us that had any respectability. And it was this, I am convinced, that saved us from being marched down to the village then and there.

Finally, after about a quarter of an hour of questions and answers, and sallies from Edgar which in the end brought a general laugh all round, we were left in freedom. The men said we could remain where we were, but must come down to the village in the morning.

We fell asleep again almost immediately, except for Kotcho, who, with great self-sacrifice and without saying a word to anyone, elected to keep himself awake in the interests of our safety, and particularly of Yolande's.

But at 5 A.M. we were somewhat brusquely called out with the words, " *Haydi, biraz kalk, bakalim* "; which is a familiar way of telling someone to get up. Two men with rifles stood over us and watched with interest as we emerged from the bags. It seemed that they had shivered all night and were not exactly pleased at having had to mount guard.

The morning was radiantly beautiful, and the first rays of light were touching with pink the uppermost summits of Olympus, while the rest of the mountain slumbered in a remote cobalt mistiness, piled up tier on tier and buttress over buttress, above the waters of the Gulf of Gemlik. I never remember a lovelier dawn.

We started in with leisurely appetites on the gargantuan dish of Birchermüsli which Edgar and I had prepared the night before, but of course we could not finish half of it, and so turned over the rest to our guards. In spite of a cordial invitation these worthies declined to have anything to do with it. Eventually, though, we prevailed on them to eat it by saying we would throw it away.

At six o'clock we were ready to go down to the village. Half-way there we met the headman, who had taken refuge for the night under a haystack. It seemed that he had not wanted to venture up to the danger zone, but had left the tracking down of the four wild people from the mountains— *i.e.*, ourselves—to the young bloods of Kumla. From the haystack onwards he plied me with questions, the most often repeated of which was, " Do you do this for money ? " He was a paunchy, not very pleasant type, dressed in town clothes ; the intense suspicion he felt towards us and disbelief of everything we said could not have been more obviously displayed.

About seven o'clock we got down to Kumla, which still bore traces of the disastrous floods of the previous September. The village is charming and typical, with its minaret and mosque, and ancient plane trees overshadowing the coffee-house. Our arrival caused a great sensation. The men stared at us as though we had come from the moon, and the women hid their faces. I doubt whether more than one foreigner in five years passes through Kumla, and certainly few can have been brought in as we were that morning.

The headman told me—a remark perhaps not bereft of innuendo—that about six months previously they had caught a wild man in the mountains who was a spy. According to the headman, " He had a beard down to his navel." What a spy should be doing on these mountains, where there are no installations even remotely military in character, was beyond my comprehension, but I thought it unwise to question the statement.

All the village crowded round to stare at us, and Edgar kept them amused by telling the story of the fire watchman and his telephone, which went down extremely well. The headman gave us coffees to drink, and conversation dragged on. Eventually I asked whether we could go back to Yalova, intending to return by the Von der Goltz route. The head-man promptly vetoed this, and said we would have to go down to the coast, where in due course a motor-boat would pass by and take us along to Gemlik ; from Gemlik we would be able to get transport to take us back to Yalova. What he did not say, but what Edgar and I understood, was that a sizable delegation of police would be waiting at Gemlik to take us into custody for more questions. Our idea received confirmation when I asked the headman if we might leave immediately by the route he proposed. All he did was to get up and say he would ask. A few moments later he returned, after making a telephone call, and said we could go.

He walked down the road with us for half a mile and then told us to get straight down to the coast. We wasted no time about this, although we had to halt a moment while I burnt my map. This seemed only sensible, because in Turkey the remnants of the old police state are still very strong ; possession of a map, which in western countries would indicate merely that you were a hiker, is sufficient here to brand you as saboteur and a spy, or at least a Communist.

We had the extraordinary good fortune to meet a coastal motor-boat carrying villagers to Gemlik just as we got to the sea, and walked straight down into it without stopping. The engine was powerful, and within a few minutes we were already half-way to Gemlik, battling through the blue waters of the Gulf in a glorious morning sun, with all the mountains we had got to know so intimately on the day before, rising on our port quarter.

The houses of Gemlik came sparkling into sight round a corner of the Gulf, and we scanned the landing-pier, not

without apprehension, for some signs of the reception com-
mittee we felt sure would be there. I got some consolation
from the thought that though I was unshaven I did not have
a beard down to my navel. But in point of fact there was
no policeman in view, nor even a plain-clothes man. We
came to the conclusion that by an odd fluke we must have
arrived in Gemlik about an hour before we were due.

Further good fortune followed. We had hardly got off
the pier when a taxi with one passenger came by soliciting
four clients for Yalova. We did not argue the price. Before
you could say knife, those four rucksacks were piled up in
the back, and we were streaking out of Gemlik at nearly
fifty miles an hour.

By 10 A.M. we were in Yalova port, and a little later at
Yalova Baths, where we sat down at the open-air restaurant
in the forest and consumed an enormous lunch supported by
massed contingents of beer bottles. The thought that by
this time half the police of Gemlik must be searching for
us, and that a state of partial mobilisation at least, for both
the army and the gendarmerie, had no doubt already been
declared, gave an added zest to the comforts of our meal,
which we might otherwise have been savouring in some
sweltering police station.

A healthy sleep in the shady glens of the Valley of Nightin-
gales followed our lunch, and we caught a ferry back to
Istanbul in the afternoon, conscious that if our expedition
had not been crowned with success, we had at least done
an interesting and even exciting trip, which was unlikely to
have been made before or repeated in the future.

And the waterfall was still there, waiting for NEXT
TIME.

CHAPTER V

TO SWITZERLAND AND THE MATTERHORN

IT had always been my ambition to visit the Alps as soon as I could afford it, for they are the goal of every mountaineer. And to all of us except those select few who are called to the Himalaya, they provide probably the greatest routes and the finest climbs that are offered to man.

I had read about the Alps since my schooldays and was already well versed in their literature, to which we as a nation have contributed perhaps more than any other. The most treasured books of my 'teens and early twenties were the books of my alpine library; and the authors whom I appreciated most were Guido Rey and Julius Kugy, together with Frank Smythe and R. L. G. Irving. But I read everything I could lay hands on, from Whymper, Sir Leslie Stephen, and Mummery onwards. In later years, when knowledge and experience were growing slowly from my expeditions in Turkey, and literary taste was ripening, one book began to stand out before all others as the epitome of mountain chivalry and romance. This was ' On High Hills,' by Geoffrey Winthrop Young, and his account of climbs like the south face of the Täschorn, and of the ability of men like Franz Lochmatter and Joseph Knubel, filled me with something like awe.

I cannot help feeling that the Alps are now more beautiful than they were a hundred years ago, and that their beauty has been heightened by the emotions of men like Guido Rey, who loved and wrote about them ; as well as by the feeling of tens of thousands of less eloquent and anonymous admirers. I think that the sensitive mind can never remain unmoved by the associations of a place, and just as some houses have a warm and welcoming atmosphere and others are cold and aloof, so it is with places whose history possesses an affecting intensity.

An early ambition had been to make my alpine début in some quiet retreat like Cogne or Binn, where an elderly guide would instil the elements of sound technique, away from the tumult of the great centres. But I was twenty-eight before I had the money for an alpine voyage, and the rumblings of strife on an uneasy planet lent a feeling of urgency to my holiday. It looked at that time as if it might even be the last opportunity to visit Switzerland, and feeling that " Some work of noble note should yet be done," I decided on one of the great centres. Guido Rey and the lure of the Matter-horn won the day. It was Zermatt. But instead of entering the sacred precincts as an expert who had served his apprentice-ship, I would be arriving as a neophyte who had never worn the rope. The impressions might be all the more vivid, but little would be left in reserve. For having once been among the Zermatt Giants, what would be left to experience that was greater or possessed a bigger wealth of tradition ? Only perhaps Mont Blanc. And in deciding for Zermatt I also decided that I would leave Courmayeur and the Montenvers to my later climbing days.

On my way to Switzerland I fell ill at Lake Como, and an anxious Italian doctor at Menaggio sat up with me part of one night to give injections and discourage me from further activity. When I told him of plans to ascend the Matterhorn he advised me to give up the thought, and added, after hearing back medical history, that my liver inflammation and gall-bladder trouble would make it impossible for me to do very much for several weeks. I lay in misery at the thought of uselessly spent savings and the leave opportunity wasted, but even during those days in bed, something told me that practically nothing is impossible provided there is enough feeling behind the wish.

Eventually the day of days came and I stood at Brigue Station awaiting the narrow-gauge train that was to take me upwards past those enchanted names that are the gateways to Paradise—Stalden, St Niklaus, Randa, and Täsch !

As we rounded the corner before Zermatt I saw what my eyes were waiting for ; and my breath was taken by the sight. The lone monolith of the Matterhorn leaps up with incredible grace and litheness, thrown high against the skies like a protest to heaven. Its shape is known to almost everyone the world over. No other mountain possesses such notoriety. None of such difficulty is scaled more often or surrounded by so much poetry or legend ; few perhaps have claimed more victims.

The early story of Zermatt is to a large extent the story of the Matterhorn and the tale of the struggle for its ascent, of Whymper's triumph and his tragedy ; with other names floating up like ghosts from the past—Carrel, whose noble end must for ever stand as an example to guides ; Tyndall, Mummery, and the " irrepressible " Guido Rey.

After reading and dreaming about it for so long, one might think that seeing it for the first time would come as an anticlimax. But this was far from the case : the towers

and cliffs that had so often flashed upon the inward eye of
fancy were even more wonderful than I had hoped.

Zermatt is no longer quite a village, and smart shops line
the main street. But it seemed to me, as a stranger, that
much of the venerable atmosphere remained, and the sense
of tradition. There were no cars in the streets and no proper
road to connect the place to Visp. The guides still sat on
their wall. The old chalets behind the hotels were weathered
and brown and mellow.

Of course the most venerable thing is the Monte Rosa
Hotel. Whymper started from there in 1865, and even to
this day the climbing atmosphere is happily preserved. There
is a pleasant sense of informality. People talk to one another
there without reserve. Fraulein Eberhardt is a mine of
information on the daily mountain doings of every inmate
and takes a personal interest in her clients. The accent is
notably English. Prints of Whymper engravings and photos
by G. P. Abrahams adorn the rooms. A rack for ice-axes
greets you as you go in. And there are wicker chairs in the
road outside.

It delighted me on first arriving to see rows and rows of
boots—few shoes—outside the bedroom doors. And sober,
serious-looking boots, lined with clinkers or tricounis. Even
the children seemed to wear them.

My favourite form of sport on the first few evenings was
to loll in a wicker chair on the road outside the Monte Rosa
and watch the returning stream of walkers and climbers.
I had never seen such people before, or such costumes.
Whereas in Turkey one went to the hills (apart from the
Uludağ) almost furtively and in constant fear of arrest, here
the tourist was obviously welcome and free. I used to try

to judge from the clothes and equipment of people as they passed, by their expression and gait, how far they had been and what category they came into ; whether they were fresh or weary, lazy or energetic, or whether they had been tired by some great climb. When I saw crampons, ropes and ice-axes, and faces scorched by the sun, I thought of glaciers and snow, and the highest places of all. Just ropes and ice-axes might mean a rock climb like the Gabelhorn or the Zinal Rothorn. And then there were the walkers carrying heavy packs but no rope, down from one of the high huts or passes perhaps. But the majority carried satchels and alpenstocks. Many were women. And some children.

As I watched the walkers and climbers streaming in down the main street of Zermatt on my first evening, and listened to the clatter of nails and the pad-pad of Vibram soles as they passed, I saluted all these people in my heart and was filled with astonishment at their numbers and at the extra-ordinary sense of life and energy that coursed down that narrow lane.

The exhilaration of finding myself in the centre of the mountaineering universe and of staying at its most sacred hostelry soon began to alter my condition. Every day I walked and explored the paths around with swiftly mounting strength. By the time I had been there a week I was feeling ready for anything and looking back gleefully on the pro-nouncements of the Menaggio doctor.

The mountains round Zermatt are felt, rather than seen. Apart from the Matterhorn and the Mischabel peaks, the eye has no evidence of the vast amphitheatre which con-centrates three-quarters of the high peaks of the Alps in a horse-shoe ring round Zermatt ; but the thunder of the

Mattervisp torrent speaks eloquently of the snowfields above. And should you ascend the slopes of larch and fir and leave the steep trough of the valley, you will see the matchless panorama of peaks and glaciers unfolding itself as you mount, until finally nothing but snow and névé, ice-falls and rocks, and the architecture of the high mountain world confront the eye. Some of the peaks are jagged spires of rock, while others like the Breithorn are crowned with domes of snow, under which the glaciers creep like old and wrinkled animals, showing an occasional blue eye of water or the glitter of ice.

I made several walks with an American lady of seventy-two called Mrs Willis, and her daughter Phyllida, who lectures in chemistry at Wellesley College, Mass. One day at the Gornergrat, when we were looking at the Bétemps Hut on Monte Rosa, Mrs Willis surprised me by saying, " I've been there, you know, to the Bétemps. It was forty years ago, with my husband. I got very tired, but I wasn't as fit and active as I am now." Few human beings could say such a thing and mean it seriously. Mrs W. meant it. She walked us right down to Zermatt at a tearing pace—all five thousand feet of the descent. Few things are more encouraging than such a demonstration of vitality by an old person.

It was with Phyllida that I used a rope for the first time. We had decided to make for the Théodule Pass guideless, and left Zermatt one morning at 5.30 A.M., bound for the Gandegg Hut. We went at a leisurely pace and enjoyed the clean air of a summer morning and the company of the great peaks around.

The Gandegg was reached at 10.30. At this height the air was cold in shadowed places, the world of civilised valleys and hotels had vanished, and the congregation of summits

filled my consciousness. We looked down on to the glaciers below Monte Rosa and the Castor-Pollux-Breithorn north faces. Below us, picking their way with slow and careful precision, was a party on the séracs of the Untertheodul-gletschev. Other parties began to drift in from the Théodul Pass. I felt this must be the authentic atmosphere of the high mountains. Tired from our walk we sat down to rest and eat.

Two and a half hours later we left the security of the shaly slabs on which the Gandegg is built, and turned south. The rocks ended. Ahead was nothing but blinding snows and glacier. I put on my goggles. We christened the one hundred and twenty foot nylon, and I was roped up for the first time. At least I knew the knots. Phyllida led, as she had already had experience in the Rockies. Fortunately for us there was a trail to follow made by other parties.

The glacier is a strange beast! And unless it is a dry glacier of naked ice, a frightening place for the neophyte. You walk on snow most of the time. But it is very different from an ordinary snowfield. For one thing, there is the feeling of perhaps a couple of hundred feet of ice beneath ; crevasses here and there, concealed by their snow covering, give an unpleasant sense of danger. Occasionally there are cracks and faults, like the fissures one sees at the epicentre of an earthquake. And a multiplicity of sound disturbs the ear. Every now and then the platter of streams is heard, flowing in rivulets near the surface, and then plunging into some chasm leading to the lower depths, whence only a muffled and subterranean gurgle ascends. The ice creaks. Little snapping and breaking noises come up from below. It is an eerie experience.

E   65

Glacier practice under the shadow of the Matterhorn

The expert would smile at the precautions we adopted on this well-worn track to the Théodule. I kept Phyllida on a tight doubled rope about fifty feet ahead, and we both of us felt quite daring. However, it is better to be safe than sorry. Mountaineering on the whole is an easy thing to do, but it can be dangerous if done badly.

We reached the Théodule Pass at about 2.15. I felt overjoyed to see the other side. We had reached the end of Switzerland; below us were the warm valleys of Italy and the lakes above Breuil. The Matterhorn had greatly altered in shape, and now displayed its Italian face with all that complexity of form and incident of ridge that has occasioned the poetic names of Col du Lion, Crête du Coq, Col Félicité, Linceul, Cravate, and others.

A hundred feet above us on the right was the Italian Rifugio di Piemonte. We scrambled up to it and met about twenty Italians lounging in the sun in various stages of undress, with skis propped up behind them. Some cheery " Buon giorno's " were exchanged, and the two frontier guards did not even ask to see our passports. We lay there and basked while two Italians played mouth-organs and the others sang quietly in harmony. Before us the immense snowfields of the Breithorn blazed against the sky. It was a jolly moment. I have seldom felt gayer. Our legs had carried us up to another land, and Phyllida and I had done our first high alpine pass.

II

Back at the Monte Rosa Hotel that night we were talking Matterhorn history and legend; the conversation ranged learnedly between the Furggen Ridge, where Guido Rey had fought and failed, and the precipices of the sunless north wall, where the brothers Schmidt had carried to success their desperate enterprise. Phyllida had satisfied her life's ambition and had been up the Matterhorn a week earlier, in the competent charge of Alfons Franzen. She introduced me to Alfons after dinner, and with slight trepidation I mentioned that it was my ambition too. Alfons asked, " You climb before ? " I replied that I never had, at which he smiled and said, "All right, I see you the day after to-morrow on Riffelhorn."

Alfons was young and extremely handsome. He had tremendous shoulders and obviously the strength of a bull. Looking back on him now with the more critical eye of experience I would not say that he was a great cragsman or in any sense a great guide, but he had a very charming personality and a good deal of patience. What is just as important, he had the gift of infusing confidence. I never at any time felt nervousness with Alfons, and if he shouted cheerfully down the line, " I hold you," there was never the slightest doubt in my mind that he could.

On the Riffelhorn we did all the things that beginners are shown, and a few of the more difficult ones. I had never been on steep rock before, but as soon as I gripped the first handholds of the Riffelhorn I felt the soaring exhilaration which has never since left me when on rock. This is not the same thing as the authentic mountain awe and the delight in the high places, but it is allied to it, and represents an important colour or part of the mountaineering spectrum. The dangers of a mechanistic attitude have often been stressed, and I count myself fortunate in some ways not to have been introduced to rock until I was nearly thirty. Those of the fraternity who have concentrated exclusively on rock-climbing have my respect. I salute them as the amateur salutes the expert; but they also have in a sense my sympathy, for I feel they have given up the greater joys.

Alfons was a conscientious mentor. He tried to show me how to make small upward movements, how to work rhythmically and keep the body swung away from the rock —and never make an effort or struggle, but just " flow " up. Beautiful in theory but hard in practice! It was made easier for me at the beginning by the feeling that Alfons had me on a tight rope; anchored always in perfect security above, he could hold, not one, but three men: if I fell I would fall at the most a couple of inches. Even so, it was difficult to overcome the natural instinct towards clinging. Sometimes Alfons would snarl good-humouredly from above, " That is not good. You tire yourself. That is not climbing." " Tire " was a word which came very often into his vocabulary. And it showed how good a teacher he was. From the physical point of view the secret of climbing lies not in strength but in smoothness; not in bulging muscles, but in the very absence of those efforts which build them.

I found climbing down the same pleasure as climbing up, and Alfons was surprised at the ease with which I negotiated rocks on the descent. " I think you do very well," he said as we sat beside the Riffelsee in the evening, with the crags of the Riffelhorn standing above us on the left. We gazed towards the Matterhorn, half-veiled by clouds, towering up across the valley: the great peak from here has the aspect almost of a spire, and one could feel on this evening that it

faced its challengers aloofly—unknowable and unknown, brooding dark and silent.

It was 30th July.

" What you say if we start to-morrow ? " asked Alfons. " I meet you at the Hörnli Hut about six. You walk up slowly from the morning."

I made a quick calculation. 1st August, on which we should therefore be climbing, was National Day, when all Zermatt is in fiesta : it would be a pity to miss the festivities through being tired out. But before I had time to object I was surprised to hear my voice say, " Splendid. I will meet you at Hörnli to-morrow night."

We careered down the three-thousand-foot descent to Zermatt in eighty minutes. My heart was pounding with excitement. Until now I had felt the challenge and the overwhelming longing to mount the Matterhorn, but also a fear of the unknown, and uncertainty whether it lay within my powers. Those giant cliffs on to which they train the telescopes in Zermatt had a forbidding grimness about them which fascinated and repelled. But now I knew, after the Riffelhorn, that I had nothing to fear : it would be the waited-for experience, and represent the satisfaction of twenty years of mountain ambitions which had slowly been crystallising to this point in space and time. The feeling was like a ray of sunlight pouring through clouds on to a valley which had been doubtfully dark before.

Fraulein Eberhardt, the charming manageress, met us at the door of the Monte Rosa. " And how did it go ? " she asked. " Fine," I replied. " To-morrow I'm leaving for Hörnli," and went upstairs to order the necessary food from Mme. Casanova. Mme. Casanova, whose autocratic rule

69

A windy sky : the Matterhorn

over the dining-room at the Monte Rosa is combined with perfect service and an indulgently helpful attitude to even the oddest requests, smiled pleasantly. " The Matterhorn, sir ; yes, of course. We will prepare special food for you and the guide " ! In her thirty years at the Monte Rosa she must have seen more climbers depart and return, and attended to their food, than almost any other person alive.

The next day I set out from Zermatt at 8.30 in the morning. After a midday lunch at the Schwarzsee Hotel (eight thousand six hundred feet up) I started on the everlasting zigzags up the shale and rock cliff to the Hörnli Belvedere. It was a warm afternoon and the roar of the glacier torrents was very loud. Below the path lay a small lake, enclosed by moraines and fed by the Furggen Glacier. Stones and ice were falling with a sporadic plonk and crash into its waters ; and the occasional grate and creak of the ice and the clatter of pebbles on the glacier made the whole scene eerily alive. The forces of rock and ice, erosion and decay, were strongly at work, with a metabolism heightened by the warm sun. Droves of climbers passed me on the way up from the Schwarzsee to the Belvedere. All the world and his wife seemed to be bound for the Hörnli. And everyone was in a hurry. I noticed despairingly the speed at which people were mounting, and wondered how I would ever do the Matterhorn in such company on the morrow.

Eventually, at 5.30 in the evening, I got to the Hörnli and stepped into the Belvedere. My room was cosy and even comfortable, with a view on to Monte Rosa and the Breithorn. At this height of ten thousand eight hundred feet the air was thin and keen ; the breeze blew sharply. One felt immensely far from Zermatt, away from all the world, set on a high ledge, and almost on a level with the great peaks themselves. The evening shadows lengthened and the sunlight on the top snows began to assume a warmer tinge.

About half-past six Alfons and another guide from Zermatt arrived. They had raced up from Zermatt in about three hours. Even Alfons seemed a bit the worse for wear.

The air grew too cold to remain out any longer, and the Matterhorn, towering up above us, had retired into menacing shadow, with only a single ice-slope on the north wall still lit by the sun. I looked up at the cliffs and pinnacles of the ridge, and then turned into the Belvedere dining-room. It was already dark in here and the room was lit by a dim lamp. People's faces looked mysterious and blurred. There was a French party, already busy consuming their supper. Two young Americans of my age and three younger Swiss lads, who seemed to form a party of five, were ensconced in one corner. A sardonic gentleman with strongly aquiline features sat silently watching us with an amused twinkle in his eyes. He was grey-haired and rather distinguished. *Un vieux loup des montagnes*, I thought.

The hostess came in and pushed the six of us into an adjoining room, where they served a large three-course supper. I ate a good deal and felt the better for it. The others ate very little. The atmosphere was one of subdued excitement. We talked hardly at all of the Matterhorn.

Alfons popped his head round the door about a quarter to eight and insisted on rushing me off to bed. He also doled out three " Pills to make sleep " in the privacy of my room and expatiated on the virtues of proper repose. I had everything laid out ready for the morrow. The water-bottle containing cold water, sugar, and Ovaltine. Chocolate in various

71

pockets. Altimeter, camera, and the rest. By the bed were matches and a candle. I lit the candle, then slipped under the sheets, hardly undressing at all.

Voices came up from the platform outside. I heard a murmur of admiration. So I got up and opened the windows. All the high snows, from the Täschorn and the Dom to the Lyskamm and the Breithorn, past the vast snowfields of Monte Rosa, were stained the most vivid pink—burning in the rays of a sun that had long departed from Hörnli and said good-bye to Zermatt in the valley a good three hours before. The sky behind was a luminous green, almost transparent, and the snows glowed like fire, as if lighted from within. I had had the luck to witness an exceptionally fine manifestation of the famous Alpine Glow. No one who has not actually seen this from high up in the mountains can have any idea of what it is like.

I took two of the tablets and sank almost immediately into a log-like sleep. At midnight I woke up and impatiently lit the candle to look at the time. Through the curtains I could see the glisten of stars. I got up to open the windows and gazed out. It was ice cold. The whole firmament sparkled with stars, vividly and sharply pricked in the black sky as I had never seen them before. There was no moon and the snows were blanched into pallor by the sole light of the constellations. Even the dark, crouching form of the Matterhorn showed snow and rock, light and shade. The world was locked in the silent rigour of frozen, windless air. Not a sound came through the night but the voice of the glacier torrent, muffled and far below.

I took the third pill and sank into another bout of sleep. At 3 A.M. there was a clattering of boots and a banging

72

of doors—hoarse voices and the sound of people blundering around in unlighted passages. I dressed in a flash, made a pretence at washing, fastened on various bits of equipment, and sped downstairs for breakfast. It was still black outside and the stars blazed with undiminished brilliance.

A veil seems to have descended over the time between three and four that morning. I remember breakfast with the two Americans and the three Swiss. Scalding coffee and rolls. The enigmatic grey-haired gentleman in the corner ; the grunted remarks about the weather and the number of ropes due to go up that day. It seemed that at least fifty people were counting to make the ascent. One of the Americans asked me how I slept, and I said, " Pretty well, thank you." There were some raised eyebrows and no one seemed to take me very seriously. It appeared that none of them had slept much, what with the height and the excitement. Naturally I refrained from mentioning Alfon's thoughtful aid to my slumbers.

At 3.30 I was ready to start, but all the guides were at Mass in the small adjoining room where we had had supper. I looked in and saw an altar by the guttering light of candles, and the muffled forms of the guides. The bells rang and the priest intoned. (Where he had come from I do not know.) Zermatt is deeply religious and strictly Roman Catholic. No guide will climb on a Sunday.

This dim nocturnal Mass somehow heightened the idea of mystery and the unknown which, perhaps from the very proximity of the Matterhorn, had enveloped everything since I arrived at the Belvedere. And now here were the guides who would shortly be leading us on the spires and ridges of the mountain, communing with God before starting. It was all a little strange and outside of ordinary experience. Almost unreal.

I descended to the kitchen, where I had a rendezvous with Alfons. He clattered down at ten to four, and got out the nylon rope from his rucksack. We roped up in the light of a solitary candle, and then stepped into the rigid coldness and silence of the night. A faint, greenish pallor was filtering over the peaks in the east, and the stars were less vivid. Dawn was breaking.

Already some parties had got ahead. A lamp was swinging thinly in front, casting a circle of orange light in the snow below the first wall of rocks. The Matterhorn loomed up, vast and almost sinister against the stars, pregnant with the unknown, with a sense of challenge, and with delight. This was the most glorious moment—before we had started; while all was dark and cold; with the Matterhorn untrodden before me. I had known always, since the age of twelve, that some day I should climb it—and now, here it was, like a date with destiny.

Alfons led on. We crossed the frozen snow, and the particles crunched musically under our feet. Then came a piece of rock and an awkward traverse to the right. It was difficult to see, and the whole caravan of parties was held up as one climber after another hesitated and struggled to worm his way round. A tight rope and a " Come on " from Alfons. I slithered past.

I cannot remember very much of the first hour after this. We were mounting swiftly and surely on easy rocks, and Alfons scarcely ever paused. We climbed in unison, apparently without precautions, and several slower parties were left behind.

74

The light grew stronger, and slowly the panorama of peaks was breathed from formless shade into the life and colour of day.

At 5 A.M. I looked up after negotiating a steeper pitch, and saw the final tower of the Matterhorn bathed in waves of orange light. It blazed like a huge torch, the only part of the visible world that had received the embrace of the sun. Even the guides paused to look. Owing to the exceptional clearness of the atmosphere the effect was more than usually vivid that morning.

We were now getting near the Solway Hut. I told Alfons we were near and gave him the height. " You know better than me," he laughed. Built after three years of strenuous efforts, the Solway lies perched in a nook on the ridge, protected from stones and wind, and only one thousand six hundred feet below the summit. It stands as a monument to the devotion and persistence of its builders, and has saved not a few lives. Only climbers in distress, or unable to get off the mountain before nightfall, are supposed to use it for sleeping.

We came to a steep and rather difficult cliff. There was an English girl in a fix at the bottom, and getting directed from above by her leader on the rope. She stepped aside courteously at the bottom to let Alfons pass. I turned and thanked her, adding, " So much traffic on the road you really need a policeman to come up here and regulate it ! "

Alfons tugged the rope. " Come on. I hold you if you fall." The rope tightened. I swung out and found myself working up easily and with little effort. " Wonderful," said Alfons. " You do wonderful well." Another few steps and we were at the Solway. Several people had already arrived and were sitting eating on the front platform. Alfons pointed to a flat rock and bade me sit down. It was a breezy position and I had never before seen slopes of such steepness and height from above.

We had taken one and three-quarter hours to the Solway, and I knew that this was very fast. After ten minutes Alfons was up. "We go now. Too many people on the mountain to-day."

After the Solway it gets more difficult. We climbed almost vertically up one of the gendarmes of the ridge, and then along the crest almost to the Shoulder. I remember vaguely a succession of spires and pinnacles, of views down on to the precipices of the North Wall, unlighted, austere and tragically cold, with frozen couloirs of vertiginous length and steepness, and the dull glisten of ice. Sometimes Alfons would stroll unconcernedly across a level tongue of rock with drops on both sides of frightening aspect. "Come on," he remarked when I hesitated, "I hold you if you fall." I would go across on all fours. "No, no, not like that," he would laugh. "Stroll along, just like you cross the street. It is so much safer."

We came to the Shoulder, perhaps the most sensational part of the climb. Above it, the final tower bounds up a clear eight hundred feet, and below, the precipices of the North Wall fall awesomely to the Zmutt Glacier. We looked across to the Furggen Shoulder, under the vast overhangs of "The Last Step"; I marvelled at the daring of men like Guido Rey and Benedetti and recalled with approval the historic decisions taken by the Mummery-Burgener and Ryan-Lochmatter-Young parties at this point. The guides were all very excited because an attempt was being made

76

"_. . . a succession of spires and pinnacles . . ._"
(_Upper Hörnli Ridge, the Matterhorn_)

on the North Wall that day, and they kept peering over the edge to see if they could make out the climbing party. But we never saw them.

All the way up Alfons had warned me about dislodging stones. With so many parties on the mountain one had to give special care to avoid sending anything down which might kill or maim those below. I paused on the Shoulder to photograph parties lower down. The American and his guide were next below us. Apparently we had outdistanced everyone else.

The first fixed rope came into view. It was on a gentle slope. Not more than 30° perhaps, but the rock was smooth and treacherous. Alfons led, and I clambered up hauling with my arms. Then more and more fixed ropes came into view, and steeper and steeper rocks. I did not care for the ropes at all, and would have much preferred to climb without them, but this would have delayed us a great deal. My arms ached. " Use your feet," said Alfons. " You tire yourself like that." Then I got the hang of it and stood almost vertically, letting the legs do most of the work on small holds.

Eventually the fixed ropes ended and the slope began to ease off. I glanced at the altimeter. Only two hundred and fifty feet to the top. Up to here I had had the sensation of floating up in an almost effortless rush of movement. My mind was outside of itself, beyond the body, buoyed up in a trance-like detachment and impervious to any quiver of fatigue. The intense joy of achievement, the feeling for beauty and physical rhythms—not unlike the sensation of dancing—had transported me to the greatest heights of elation. But finally the thin, rarefied atmosphere began to tell on the lungs. More breaths were needed to accomplish the same movements. Alfons pressed on. We passed thin flakes of snow and ice.

Then a long sweeping ridge of snow, shaped like a scimitar and fluted to a sharp edge of ice, hove into view.

The summit ridge of the Matterhorn.

All those who tread these last two hundred yards of snow, thrown high into the sky, isolated from all the other great peaks, and hung far above the world, know the exhilaration of a great moment ; but for me standing there as a beginner on his first peak there was also the satisfaction of a dream realised.

We got into the snow and mounted the path beaten down on the Swiss side. This is a few feet from the knife-edge of ice overlooking the precipices of the Italian face. On the ultimate point of the ridge a solitary female figure and her guide were calmly munching their second breakfast. " Felicitations," I shouted, and waved our greetings to them. Alfons took my hand. " You have done wonderful well," he said; " I congratulate you."

We retraced our steps to the eastern summit and sat down to eat on some flat rocks overlooking the Italian side. It was now half-past seven, and we had reached the top at 7.25, less than three hours and a half after leaving the Belvedere.

The view was one of extraordinary breadth and completeness. The air was so brilliantly clear that I think some of the peaks in Italy which we saw must have been over one hundred and fifty miles away. I turned to Alfons and pointed out the principal peaks to him questioningly : Mont Blanc ? the Dent d'Hérens ? Dent Blanche ? Weisshorn ? Jungfrau,

Eiger, Mönch ? Finsteraahorn ? " I knew their shapes and positions already so well from maps and photos that it was not very difficult. Mont Blanc looked so close that you could almost lean over and touch it ; the more we gazed the farther we realised we could see, until we relapsed into silence, without further comment.

The American, with his guide, Emil Perren, joined us, and then we saw more and more climbers crowding up behind. I remember the American eating an orange and spitting out the pips. "One for Italy and one for Switzerland," he kept saying as they left his mouth, alternatively left and right over the Italian and Swiss sides.

We remained on the summit for almost three-quarters of an hour. The prisms of light poured down from the sky, and the vault of space above was deepened to a rich and lonely blue. Around us stood the immense congregation of peaks, pointing their upper snows whitely into the regions where now we sat ; the lower glaciers and valleys slumbered in a haze of thicker air. Even Zermatt seemed only a memory, part of the different world of plains. The clear, sword-like brilliance of the summits filled my mind. I knew the fullness of living. I had climbed the Matterhorn.

On the descent, being first down, I thought that I would perhaps have the satisfaction of making the route. But Alfons had a proper sense of his responsibilities, and constantly gave directions. " Left . . . Right . . . Traverse " or " Be careful."

We came to the fixed ropes again and here met a number of slower parties still coming up. I went down the ropes at a good rate, sideways to the rock, with the body almost horizontal, which was quite wrong. After I had reached a stance Alfons would follow in a series of tigerish leaps. The rope seemed barely to touch his hands, and he would sweep down from ledge to ledge with a " Zomp—Swish—Zomp " of his Vibram rubber soles, descending perhaps five times as fast as I.

The procession of spires and outcrops on the ridge handed us on from one to the next ; I remember finding them quicker to overcome than on the way up. A final pitch before the Solway caused some delay and then we unroped and entered the hut about an hour after leaving the summit. The air was warm in this windless and sheltered corner ; the rays of the sun falling untempered through the upper atmosphere made it too hot to remain outside on the platform. Alfons and I entered and sat down at the table inside. " Here we have a rest," he said. " You come down very fast." The Solway has benches round a table and bunks for six or eight people. A plaque commemorates its builders. I felt satisfaction at being somewhere I had read so much about, and my mind went back to all those climbers who had found salvation from wind and weather within these narrow walls. Half an hour passed very agreeably before we roped up and took off for the remainder of the descent to the Belvedere.

Presently we were at the ruins of the old Solway Hut, amid a débris of loosely tilted slabs and rock. Alfons enjoined caution. I looked down to the glacier below and understood why. Beneath us stretched a shallow couloir, and the whole of its surface was coated with a thick powdery scum of yellow dust left by rocks as they had crashed their way down. The ice at the bottom was pitted with blocks of stone, and spattered with the filth of boulders and rubble. It was a sinister sight.

We passed by and were soon on the easier rocks leading

The Untergabelhorn from the we

to the Belvedere. In the light of day I could now see almost a path going down through the crags. An hour and twenty minutes after leaving the Solway we were once more standing on the Belvedere platform amid a throng of gazers through the telescope, and visitors who had walked up from Zermatt. A cloud had veiled the top of the mountain, and a fresh breeze was sweeping across from the west. Apart from aching shoulders I was untired.

At the Schwarzsee on the way down to Zermatt I met Canon Thornhill, the warmth of whose greeting gave me more pleasure than the combined congratulations of the other company at the hotel. More than anyone else he had encouraged me to sally forth; for with the intuition of a spiritual personality he had divined all there was to know without being told.

That evening was gala night, in celebration of Swiss National Day. The Monte Rosa put on a special menu. There were flowers everywhere, and lanterns burning. Every window and balcony was decorated with lights. Miss Eberhardt and Mme. Casanova welcomed me back to the fold with appropriate satisfaction.

Before we had got to the end of our meal the fireworks started outside; then a procession of all the citizens of the commune went by carrying Chinese lanterns on sticks, and walking behind their band. Roman Candles were popping off in the Zermatterhoff Gardens. On the hilltops and crags above Zermatt bonfires were burning; coloured illuminations had even been put into the cliffs behind the village—some of them over a thousand feet up.

There was a ball at the Victoria Hotel to which I went, and I danced amidst an atmosphere of infectious carouse

F

until half-past one. After twenty-three hours on my feet and efforts which would have seemed unimaginable before, I reached my bed at the Monte Rosa at 2 A.M. The four-thousand-foot climb and the nine-and-a-half-thousand-foot descent seemed to have made very little physical impression —striking proof that feeling, if sufficiently intense, can reverse the natural laws and extend almost indefinitely the margin of the possible. Perhaps, though, feeling of this kind only comes once or twice in a lifetime.

III

My partner at the Victoria Hotel on National Night was Jean Richards, and before she left Zermatt she introduced me to Edward Pugliese. Edward had apparently been stay-ing some months at the Monte Rosa, a lonely, almost for-bidding figure. One saw very little of him, for his walks and climbs were usually done in splendid isolation. One evening he showed me some of his photographs. The moment I saw the pictures I felt I would like to get to know him. For here was mountain photography of outstanding beauty, and the quantity of the work as well as its quality filled me with admiration.

Edward will always remain a mysterious figure. To this day I do not know precisely what he did in life. It seemed that he lived in New York. That his nationality was American I could see from his passport; but his manners were altogether the most courteous and the most polished I have ever met with. Only a man with an Italian background could have carried them off and still charmed you. With delicate reticence he fended off all attempts to find out more about him, and we met only on the level of photography and mountains. He had a background of many peaks, and when a young man had ascended some of the severest walls in the Dolomites.

One saw him rarely at the Monte Rosa. He was usually out all day and only appeared for an early dinner. I gathered that he sometimes started as early as 2 A.M., and wandered round with his camera looking for dawn on high peaks, or trying to capture the streaming mists of early morning on a ridge—always seeking for the unattainable, ideal photo which exists only in the world of the mind.

He was strongly built and dark, with keen brown eyes and an aquiline nose. There was a certain severity in his features. His movements were rhythmical and slow, and his climbing stride cautiously controlled, with a suggestion of hidden power behind it. From our first few conversations I thought of him more as a photographer than a climber, but after our joint expedition it was clear that the feeling which sent him out day after day on his solitary quests to the hills, was the ardour of a born mountaineer.

One night he told me in his cautious, rather reserved way that the Gabelhorn Ridge would offer unparalleled chances for photography, and that he had been trying for weeks to force a way up to it from the Distelgufe basin. To my diffident suggestion for a combined assault from the Distelgufe he seemed at first dubious, but he accepted when I said how much I would enjoy going out with another photographer who would not mind spending half an hour on one photo.

We set out from Zermatt at half-past four in the morning; in the desertion of night the village looked spectrally muted and quiet. The air was motionless and dead, rather warm and heavy. Stars showed thinly here and there among woolly layers of cloud, and as we mounted the first windings of the Trift path I began to have my doubts about the weather.

The first rays of the sun lit the Breithorn just as we reached the craggy platform of the Edelweiss Hotel, a thousand feet above Zermatt, but clouds were clinging sombrely to the lower ridges. From the Edelweiss we took the Hohlicht path, and continued on, hour after hour, always upwards. Edward was mounting in his slowest rhythm, and I think our speed was hardly a thousand feet an hour.

The Distelgufe is an old glacier basin under the Gabel-horn Ridge ; it is surmounted on three sides by a cirque of cliffs. Edward had tried no less than six times to force one or other of the couloirs leading up to the ridge, but he had always been beaten back. It was not a regular route and none of the Zermatt guides seemed to know the place. To get to the Distelgufe we had climbed endless screes and moraines and clambered over innumerable blocks. It was not a pretty way. By 11.30 though we were at the base of the cliffs, under the Gabel Ridge, with the last remnants of the dying glacier gurgling below us. Here we put on the rope.

Edward led, and after an easy climb we got to the base of a narrow couloir perhaps two hundred feet high, leading straight up. This was the crux of the day. If we could surmount the couloir the rest was easy.

It took us just an hour to do that two hundred feet, and Edward led them most nobly. We had to hoist the rucksacks separately to a stance, and it was quite a manœuvre to do this without damaging them. I was in doubt whether we would get through or not, and Edward did not know himself until about six feet from the top, when through the embrasure

84

of the wall he saw the glare of snows just above him. For once he forsook his usual calm and shouted down : "It's in the bag!"

As I pulled myself up the last few feet and stepped on to a platform of rock, Edward grabbed me by the hand, his face alight with pleasure. The ridge was ours, and not a footprint about to show that anyone had been there.

We were eleven thousand feet up. The time was ten past two. Clouds were boiling round the Zinal Rothorn, and the air we were breathing was inert and lifeless, with a menacing stillness and warmth about it. On the Matterhorn a storm was gathering, and the growl of ice avalanches came to our ears from the North Wall.

The ridge was sharp and dazzlingly white, with outcrops of rock jutting through the snow. It led in a series of short sweeps to the peak of the Untergabelhorn, which lifted its challenging tower ahead of us in the east. On both sides the slopes fell away steeply. The views were tremendous. Behind us, the Obergabelhorn and the Wellenkuppe. On the other side, the Zinal Rothorn and the Trifthorn. We were on a tongue of high rocks running between the great peaks. I could understand now the determination that Edward had shown to get here. The place was a photographer's dream. And the stormy weather—clouds and sun—made a perfect background to the mountains. We got the cameras out and started work.

Every now and then the thunder of an avalanche echoed round the circuit of peaks, through the flat sultry air. There seemed to me in the atmosphere to be something like expectancy; as if the universe were trembling on the brink of some revelation which was yet withheld. My faculties have seldom been more awake, or the awareness more vivid and complete. I looked at the Untergabelhorn. How wonderful to climb it ! And from the wrong side, too.

" What about it ? " I asked. Edward hesitated. I could see a struggle in his mind. Finally his caution prevailed over his natural impulse and he replied, " A bit risky now. We'd better wait and see what the weather is going to do."

The sky began to darken soon after that, and we saw that the storm on the Matterhorn had developed. A gust of wind came up at us, and the clouds moved forward. We sat down on a rock and waited for it. Raindrops fell. Then hail. The wind tugged at the ridge and I began to shiver. Then, quite suddenly it was over. The sun peered through again.

We started.

Edward led cautiously, sounding here and there with his axe. Occasional concealed crevasses underlay the soft snow, but by walking near to the very crest we made respectable progress. There is nothing more exhilarating than a high ridge, one side in sun, the other in shade.

We reached the rocks of the Untergabelhorn and started swinging up the slabs of this sombre peak. Compared with our struggles in the couloir it seemed relatively benign. But after the first summit one had to tread an exposed tongue with sensational drops on both sides, in order to get to the highest point. It was an interesting step. I can still remember the surge of excitement and pleasure as I tackled it—and Edward's paternal smile.

It was 4.30 when we were up, and no sooner did we reach the summit than we saw another storm gathering behind us. After a couple of hasty photos I was scurrying down again

86

at full speed, with Edward paying out the sixty-foot length of doubled rope, an expression half amused, half anxious on his usually imperturbable face.

It looked very threatening at one moment, but then the weather changed suddenly, as it can in the mountains, and the clouds began to dissipate. The storm blew over.

In half an hour we were back again at our couloir of the morning. I stuffed my axe in the rucksack and descended on a single rope ; then unroped and let Edward come down *en rappel*. We reached the Distelgufe at 6.30, and eight o'clock saw us near the Hohlicht path again.

The great peaks had retired into the hush of a cloudy twilight. Odd shafts of light lingered on the ribs of the Matterhorn North Face, and lit with garish contrasts the rocks and ice of this mighty wall.

The air was still mild.

We sat down and had a little food.

Fifteen and a half hours had passed since we left Zermatt, and I began to notice the sensation of tiredness ; not acute or pronounced, but muffling somewhat that spring of each movement, and relaxing the gait to a less purposeful rhythm. Edward was rather more tired.

When we got up it was becoming dark, and the Hohlicht path was difficult to follow. Clouds shut out the stars. We walked slower and slower, sometimes stumbling. Neither of us had a torch, and the strain of intense searching for the way ahead began to tire us more than all the efforts of the day.

Edward wanted to descend to the Trift Inn and spend the night there, but I was obstinately bent on making the Monte Rosa, more than two thousand feet lower. Eventually

I decided he was right, and we took the Trift path. Towards the end I noticed a great sluggishness in the limbs; my legs would not answer the brain messages very quickly. The rucksack might have been full of stones, so heavy had it become. Edward was also greatly worn and said he could not have done much more. We had been going for over seventeen hours.

It took us some time to wake them up at the Trift, but we got our beds finally. I slept on the floor because my bed was too short.

The next day we raced down to Zermatt through early morning mists, without a trace of stiffness or fatigue anywhere. The Trift Gorge sparkled with colours, and the rocks shone cleanly through the diffused sunlight, as if they had been scrubbed in the night. Zermatt seemed all bustle and activity; the streets rang to the clink of nails and boots, and a hot morning sun poured its rays into the village.

They had been worried at the Monte Rosa, and Miss Eberhardt and the porter welcomed us back with considerable relief. As for Mme. Casanova, she went so far as to prepare a special breakfast for us well after the usual time.

IV

The holiday in Zermatt was drawing to its close; only a few days were left and I spent most of my time round Findelen, either sketching or taking photos. The last morning but one I occupied myself with step-cutting practice on the snout of the Findelen Glacier; then repaired to the Grünsee for a distinctly cold bathe.

As I lay in the sun afterwards I watched a stealthy array

of clouds swinging up over the Rothorn-Gabelhorn Ridge. The warmth of the sun's rays slowly oozed away, and I saw the whole array of peaks and glaciers gradually mist over like the image in a mirror which has been breathed on.

Before I reached Zermatt the weather had broken. A cold wind roared across from the Trift, and rain was slashing down through the larch forests. In the evening the wind turned to a gale and the air became like ice.

Next morning all the slopes were covered with new snow. The Matterhorn stood out in a radiant, shimmering cloak of whiteness. The wind was north, and plumes of snow crystals were being blown off the Furggen Ridge and the Shoulder. No one got up that day.

I spent my time packing and taking a few last photos. It was bitterly cold.

In the frosty air of the following morning I left Zermatt at a time when the sun had not yet risen. Miss Eberhardt was up to see me off, and the porter trundled my things down to the station in his little trolley. " You'll be coming back ? " they both asked.

As I walked down the street my breath rose white against the dark timbers of the houses, and I thought I had never seen the village so vivid and alert, so cold and clear and sharp. It was a morning for great climbs and swift walking. In an hour the street would resound to the clatter of boots and nails, and life would flow into the veins of this historic place; the urgent, exhilarated—even ecstatic—sense of life that from the days of Whymper and Tyndall has sent generation after generation of climbers up to the freedom of the rocks and the splendour of the snows. The ghosts of the early pioneers seemed very close at hand that morning.

CHAPTER VI

THE SNOW-LEDGE ON THE DK

THIS is the story of a journey in South Turkey to the remotest parts of the Taurus Range ; and of the adventure we had there.

Originally there were four of us in the party, and we had a date to meet on 6th October in the ancient town of Cæsarea (now Kayseri). Two companions and myself were to arrive by express from Istanbul. The fourth member of the group was coming in from the eastern provinces of Turkey, after a long and audacious journey through the Russian and Persian border areas. This was Pauline, whose solitary trip from Rize to Van was the first of its kind ever to be undertaken by a lone girl.

Owing to an unfortunate series of accidents, the two other Istanbul members of the party were forced at the last moment to drop out, and it was impossible to get into touch with Pauline to inform her. After a good deal of hesitation, and after missing the express, I eventually decided to chance things and fly down to Kayseri in the hope that it would still be possible to carry out the original plan. So I booked a passage on the plane of 7th October.

Up to now we had been having unbroken summer in Istanbul, but the dawn of 7th October was forbiddingly grey. My outside thermometer showed a startling drop in temperature, and masses of cloud were pouring down from the Black Sea before a wind that set the waves foaming on the Bosphorus. There was even some doubt about the plane leaving, but eventually a reassuring signal came in from Ankara and we took off from Istanbul airport about 8.30 A.M.

An hour and forty minutes of flying takes one from Istanbul across the mountains and forests and plateaux of Anatolia to the high capital city of Ankara. Here I changed aircraft and boarded the Kayseri plane.

We were still among the concrete runways and tidy architecture of the capital, but as soon as I stepped into the other plane I had a pleasant feeling as if some adventure lay ahead and the trappings of civilised life were being left behind. Instead of business men in smart suits, these passengers looked leaner and harder ; they had tanned and leathery features that bespoke a life under the hot suns and bitter blizzards of the eastern plateau. Some had peasant coats on, and two wore fur caps. It was a different world.

Kayseri was swathed in cloud, and we bumped down on to a landing-strip that looked like a field. As I stepped out of the plane a gust of wind that felt as if it had just left Siberia nearly tore my coat away. The lower slopes of the Erciyas Dağ (Mount Argeaus) were all smothered in new snow, and the only pleasant sight to meet the eye was Pauline's cheerful figure striding up, which told me that the cable I had sent to the Chief of Police in Kayseri had been safely delivered to her.

She was very surprised to find me alone, but agreed to going through with our plans, come weal come woe. Ever since she came to Turkey three years previously on a Foreign Office contract, Pauline had wanted to climb Ararat, a mountain of mysterious appeal, remote and difficult to approach, sealed by cordons of military zones, and greater than anything in the Alps, with its clear slope of fourteen and a half thousand feet arising above the plateau in one huge sweep from the orchards of Iğdir to the icy cone of its summit. But when finally she got permission to visit the region, lack of time and the absence of a climbing companion made it impossible to achieve the dream of being the first woman up there. Starting from Istanbul, Ararat would demand a full three weeks' holiday to ascend and I had countered by proposing the Demirkazik.

This outstanding peak is the queen of the Taurus Range, and soars up like a great battering-ram or pile, rising over twelve thousand feet into the skies of Southern Turkey. In fact the word " Demirkazik " means just that—" Iron Pile " —and the name had always exercised a fascination over me. So far as I knew, only four ascents, and all of them in summer, had so far been made. 1950 seemed a good year to start a new enterprise, and the DK, as we called it, seemed a worthy goal; Pauline had accepted it as a good second-best to Ararat.

There was a day and a half to wait before we could continue our journey to the Taurus, and we wandered round the old walls of Cæsarea looking at the Hittite remains and browsing in the Turkish market, with one eye always cocked on the weather. It remained bitterly cold—in a most un-seasonable manner—and clouds veiled the Argeaus so that we never saw much beyond the foothills. At last, on the evening of 8th October, the sky cleared and we went to bed at 9 P.M. with more hopeful feelings. Four hours later we were up again and packing equipment to catch the 2.07 A.M.

train to Niğde. Besides the normal kit I had my ice-axe and a hundred-foot length of nylon rope, as well as three sleeping-bags and a string-bag full of food.

The train was packed with soldiers and incredibly dirty. We did not sleep. Eventually dawn came over the Anatolian plateau, and we saw a cold, remote sky of ethereal green, deepening to gold and then to orange, behind the distant snowy shapes of the Taurus peaks. The ground was frozen hard, and the sparse bushes carried haloes of hoar-frost.

We came to Niğde in the brightness of early morning, and found a porter to carry our bags up from the railway station to the Seldjuk walls and minarets of the town. Our arrival caused a great sensation at the local eating-house, which was named, gaily enough, " The Restaurant of Spring." With ravenous appetites we got out the bacon I had brought from Istanbul and ordered a right royal breakfast. Pauline invaded the kitchen and fried the bacon and eggs herself, over a range of wood-fires and in an atmosphere of thick smoke. The cook inquired what the strangely striped fatty meat was, and we had to tell him in a slightly diffident manner, using the phraseology proper to such an explanation, " It is, if you'll excuse our mentioning the fact, pig-flesh."

After breakfast we went to call on the Vali, or Governor, of the province of Niğde. Although the town has only about eleven thousand inhabitants, it is the capital of a large province. A Vali is an extremely important official, and his powers are very wide. Pauline always believed in going to the top.

The Vali gave us an affable welcome, and after initial courtesies he inquired how we were proposing to get to the Demirkazik. This was just the opening we were awaiting.

93

There was no way that we knew of except a somewhat dubious track about forty miles long which was said to be unmotorable. After making sure we really wanted to get to the remote township of Chamardi, not far from the base of the Demirkazik, the Vali despatched one of his officers to round up all the lorry-drivers and busmen who might be going near there. Eventually one ragged and trembling driver was marched in, aghast at being summoned to the Vali's office. The Vali said, " Where are you going ? " and the driver mentioned some other village, to which the Vali replied, " You will take these people to Chamardi, and they will pay you three liras each" (about eight shillings). That was all. No argument. The driver retired bowing.

The old rattle-trap of a bus was supposed to leave at eleven, but at the last moment the Kaymakam (or Mayor) of Chamardi decided that he would travel with us, and kept the assembled busful of people waiting two and a half hours while he had his lunch and chatted with friends.

The road to Chamardi is appalling. Most of the time we seemed to be wandering up trackless hillsides or weaving in and out of boulders across open country. At every small village there was a lengthy halt while " His Highness " the Kaymakam held court, in regal manner, with everyone bowing and scraping before him. Finally, after many hours of jolts, bangs and creaks, which sometimes made one think the bus would fall altogether to pieces, we came over a rise and saw before us, suddenly revealed, a huge wall of mountains, with jagged peaks sawing at the sky, and snows stained faintly pink in the evening light. It was one of those moments which impress by finding the watcher un-prepared for them. We recognised the Demirkazik at once from the photographs we had seen. There it was, with its great northern precipices in frigid shade, and lofty towers and battlements guarding the west face. It was a sight to quicken any climber's heart. And the weather was clear.

Day changed into night, and we descended to the valley at the base of the mountains. The Kaymakam stopped the bus at a point near a village called Chukur Bağ and said that, while we would be welcome at Chamardi, he suggested our getting off here because it was nearer to the peaks. We unfolded stiffened limbs and hobbled out. I was particularly pleased to leave the bus because a stray spring had come through the seat and the coil had been engaged in boring a hole through my trousers for the last hour or more.

Two or three peasants also going to Chukur Bağ left the bus, and the Kaymakam gave orders to the senior of them, a man called Abdullah Aygün, that we were to be properly looked after. The village was on the other side of the Gürgün Su valley, across a twenty-five or thirty foot river, and Abdullah bawled out into the night for " animals " to come over and get us. After some minutes we heard bells and a troop of donkeys came out of the darkness towards us. The various bags and equipment were loaded up, and we set off down a steep path to the sound of rushing waters. The passage of the river filled me with apprehension. There are pleasanter forms of entertainment than crossing a twenty-five-foot torrent on a donkey in the night, especially when you are carrying a heavy rucksack, but Pauline, clutching her new Contax to her bosom, did not seem to mind a bit.

We arrived at the village about half-past seven, and were immediately ushered by Abdullah into the Principal's house. This was composed of a single room with an earth floor covered

95

by home-spun rugs, and no furniture except a lot of cushions round the sides. A dim tallow lamp supplied an uncertain light. It was obviously the correct thing to remove one's shoes, and Pauline and I padded across in stockinged feet towards a couple of cushions where we were asked to sit. Practically the whole village crowded in to gaze at us with unconcealed astonishment, even some of the women and children. These, however, had to remain standing, and they were very quickly shooed out, some with cuffs on the head; as were also the young men. No one was allowed to address us except the elders, who welcomed us with ornate courtesy that taxed even Pauline's remarkable knowledge of Turkish idiom to find the suitable rejoinders.

We were plied with innumerable questions, almost the first of which was, " What is your rank and what salary do you earn ? " Pauline said she was a woman official of a foreign embassy, with pay that was " Not fixed," while I was a business man whose yearly profits were " Uncertain." We were then asked which of us was " Stronger at reading and writing," and had to reply that our attainments in these difficult arts were approximately equal. At last they inquired if we would like to eat. When we said yes a three-legged stool was brought in and turned upside down. On this our friend Abdullah put a tray, and we were offered sickly sweet warm milk, apples, and wafer-thin flaps of very salt wet bread, rolled out rather like pancakes a foot in diameter. It was not an easy meal to cope with, and hardly the best food for a major physical effort on the morrow. I thought longingly of the string-bag, but we felt it would be impolite to do anything about it.

Our day had started at I A.M. and we were half asleep

from weariness ; but it was only with difficulty that we got our hosts to realise that what we wanted more than anything else was a place to go to bed.

Meanwhile arrangements had been made for Abdullah's brother, Neshet Aygün, to call the next morning at 6.15 with donkeys and take us as far as possible on our way. Everyone had well-meant advice to give about routes, and Neshet said he would show us where the German climbers had started from some years previously. I did not care much for this idea, because Edward Peck of the Alpine Club had written to tell me that they spent thirty-two hours getting up the south-west ridge. The best plan seemed to be to make a careful reconnaissance by daylight on the morrow, and then go straight ahead by our own route while the good weather lasted.

We were taken to another house to sleep. Once again, an earth floor, covered by a few rugs. There were two mattresses with coverlets laid on either side of a mud fireplace where a blaze of twigs crackled cheerfully. The sight was balm to our tired heads, and after shooing away some curious hangers-on we got out a couple of sleeping-bags and lost no time piling into them.

I was up at dawn the next day, and roused a lethargic Pauline just in time to get her out before a whole crowd of villagers came trooping in, including Abdullah, and a certain Mustafa Güler, who owned the house where we had slept. Mustafa was a dignified man, with aquiline features and a moustache, and was obviously held in great esteem by the village. He looked a little reproachfully at the sleeping-bags and remarked, " You need have no fear of bugs or lice in my house. I am a widower, and there has been no wife or

G   97

children here to make dirt for the last fourteen years." I was to remember this sentence with peculiar force on the following evening, but thought little of it at the time.

Abdullah put twigs in the fireplace and soon got a fire going. Tea was brewed in a tiny coffee-pot, and hot water separately. We were given very sweet hot tea, and more of that atrocious " bread." Pauline showed wonderful composure, but I was anxious to get away, and rapidly losing all patience with the overpowering matutinal courtesies of which we were being made the object. To fritter away in this manner the hallowed minutes which follow dawn seemed little short of sacrilege. Eventually Neshet and his donkeys arrived, a whole hour late.

It was 7.15 and the sun was high. But at last, at long last, we were off and going to climb the DK. The morning was frosty, but radiantly fine—and the sky blue, almost violet in its clearness. Not a twig stirred. We topped a rise with poplars at the crest ; and there it was ahead of us —a vast pile of rock leaping into the sky, buttress over buttress and tower on tower, silhouetted sharply against the eastern skies.

The donkeys were laden with my big rucksack, Pauline's rucksack, the string-bag, and—tell it not in Gath—three sleeping-bags stuffed into a Foreign Office diplomatic bag. Neshet and his little son prodded on the donkeys and we made a fair pace.

The way led over gentle slopes and rolling country, with the DK face looming ever closer in front of us. The nearer we got, the less steep and pointed it looked, until finally the uppermost towers began to settle down behind their humbler brethren. Before this happened I called a halt and spent many minutes searching the rocks with my binoculars. Eventually I decided on a route leading up a wide shallow gully, broken by many subsidiary clefts and couloirs, which takes up most of the west face of the mountain. This way had an advantage in that we would be able to take the donkeys up pretty high. Pauline agreed with the choice, and after laments from the donkey-driver whose conservative heart was fixed on the "*Alman Effendiler*" and their south-west ridge, we continued on our way.

An hour later, after outflanking the rock escarpment, we had reached the highest tongue of earth leading into the heart of the DK. It was 11.15 and my altimeter showed a height of eight thousand six hundred and fifty feet—about four thousand feet above Chukur Bağ. The donkeys were unsaddled and Neshet and the little boy got out a large water-melon which they proceeded to carve in an artistic manner. Our string-bag contained butter, cheese, jam, apples, a tin of soup, some chocolate, and a couple of tommy cookers. Everything was perfect except that there was no bread and no meat. We had never yet been to a place where they did not make bread, and although I had considered buying some in Niğde, we had decided in the end not to bother. This was a great mistake. The salt, wet "pancaky" flaps which Neshet had brought were a poor substitute for the staff of life and made it difficult to consume our other food. However, we made some sort of a meal, and then stretched out and rested.

The sky above us was blue with an intensity of colour I had never seen anywhere before, and the blaze of light shining down from the sun had a strange and almost unreal brilliance. In the shade it was cold—a stabbing cold that froze the wetness in every crack. Behind us we could see slabs and pinnacles, stretching up illimitably to yet farther and steeper slabs, picked out ultimately in strident whiteness against the deep dome of the sky. I looked for snow, but could see practically none. This was odd. The evening before, the whole face had seemed covered in a fresh coating.

The time came to start. Part of the food was transferred to our rucksacks. I packed all my gear, put the rope over my shoulders, and we were off. Neshet gallantly agreed to accompany us for an hour and carry the F.O. bag with the sleeping-things. Pauline and I swung into rhythm and mounted slowly, while Neshet went dancing on ahead like a mountain goat, scrambling up the slabs in his fur-soled slippers with the zest of a boy. At every jutting rock he would stop and look down at us, an amused expression on his wrinkled face, until we had caught him up.

The scrambling got more difficult. We came to flecks of snow, then wider patches, and finally whole sheets of whiteness veiling the rock below us. Neshet came to a projecting slab and sat down. This was as far as he would go. The donkeys were now away beneath us, three barely discernible dots below our feet. We unpacked the sleeping-bags. I took the two heavier ones, and Pauline stuffed the kapok bag into her own rucksack. We shook hands with Neshet and then watched his slight retreating form descending the rock with the easy movements of a hillsman. He was going back that night to a mud-hut village in the valley, and would return for us on the morrow.

Seeing how easy it had been so far, I proposed to Pauline that we should modify the earlier plan of bivouacking in a sheltered place at about ten thousand five hundred feet and

instead climb right up to the summit that same afternoon.
" We can sleep on the peak. It will be quite an experience,"
I added hopefully. Pauline gave me a withering glance.
" I always thought you weren't quite right in the head,
but this clinches it."

She agreed all the same !

The rucksacks were bulging, and to say that mine felt
heavy was a distinct understatement. But we started up.
The slope of the great gully was steepening all the time,
and the slabs were inclined downwards like the tiles on a
roof. This was why the snow had been hidden. We had
only been able to see the edges of the tiles, not their surface,
from below. Pauline was wearing trousers and using clinker
nailing, while I had boots with Dufour rubber soles. Balance
was becoming delicate, and we moved with constant care and
attention over easy rocks to which in dry weather I would
hardly have given thought.

The sky had now darkened to an intense azure of the
deepest and coldest hue, and the rocks above us were
riven into a series of gaunt crags and frowning pinnacles.
I saw to the right a couloir which looked climbable, and
which was apparently free from ice and snow. In this gully
seemed to lie the key to the whole ascent. The going above
looked easier, and if we could climb it there seemed a good
chance that the DK was ours. If not, we should have to
retreat, at any rate for that day.

I led up and up. Over snowy slabs and glazed slabs,
by small icy cracks and gullies, but as much as possible
on the occasional narrow ribs which afforded better footing.
A declining sun hung low in the west, and the silver thread
of the Gürgün Su shone far beneath us in the valley.

Demirkazik : looking down from near the snow-ledge

The sense of isolation and withdrawal was complete now. Neshet and the donkeys were far away, beyond recall, and we were committed to a "Night on the Bald Mountain." It was different somehow from what one had felt in Switzerland, where there were huts and guides and always the chance of meeting another party. No one had been on the DK for many years, and probably no human being had ever before trodden the rocks where now we mounted. One had an exhilarated feeling of mastery over fate and detachment from every mortal care. Nothing existed but the DK and our two selves.

We saw, away to the west, the panoply of peaks and plains stretching past the snowy cone of the Argeaus, and fading into the hazes of the Anatolian Plateau. To the thick air of the valleys the evening sun had given a warmer tinge, while the high places remained cold and blue and withdrawn, like sentinels guarding a lost world; and behind them extended the azure sky of that same incredible depth and clarity that suggested the dark void of interstellar space.

We turned and attacked the rocks leading to the base of my couloir. The ice glittered. A few chips with the axe and a long pull brought us gradually up. We had reached the base. But we were in a narrow spot; and while the summit of the gully was bathed in warm sunlight, the lower end lay in hooded shade, silent and gloomy. All round were steep rocks and pinnacle walls. It was a hostile, vertical world. We began to see that the DK was not so easy as we had imagined—at least by this route and under bad conditions.

The ledge was narrow, and I scrambled up a few feet to see what the couloir looked like. Further inspection was depressing. The place was like a narrow funnel, choked with loose snow. And underneath was ice. In these dark walls there seemed to reign a tragic cold which had been there since time began. The sound of my movements was muffled and one felt a compulsion to silence. My fingers swelled and became hard and numb with the cold, until they appeared to belong to another body.

I brought Pauline up on the rope, and wedged her so that she was well placed, then tried to beat some sensation back into my hands.

Our fortunes had now greatly altered. Five minutes earlier we had been climbing in complete safety on awkward but not very steep slabs, with fingers warm in an evening sun. The altimeter had shown above eleven thousand feet, and perhaps only an hour separated us from the top. But now it was a very different story. It is easy to say afterwards, " Why didn't you get out your gloves and take off the rucksack so as to haul it up on the rope ? " The fact was, it was virtually impossible, in my position, to make such a manœuvre without considerable danger ; and to descend would have involved a delay we could not afford. We had our eyes on the sun and on our watches. A bare hour of daylight remained, and only about half an hour until the sun was to dip below the plateau rim. I made a quick decision. We would continue the climb.

Pauline paid out the rope as I inched up the couloir, mostly on pressure holds, hoping always that the ice would end and I would see above me the warm rocks bathed in the orange light that seemed to be the talisman of our enterprise. I had ascended about twenty-five or thirty feet and there seemed to be only another ten or so to do before the slope eased off to a ledge below the top rocks of the couloir, when disaster came. My rucksack got securely jammed.

" I'm stuck, Pauline ! " I shouted. " Can't get up or down." " Well, get down then," said Pauline with truly feminine logic. The position was awkward. My fingers had become quite numb again and I felt they would not support the effort of hanging on while a downward movement of the body was made to free the rucksack. It seemed to be only a question of time before I should drop off, for the strain, once movement had stopped, was considerable.

" The chances are, I shall fall off," I remarked cheerfully. " What are you going to do about it ? " " I can hold you," said Pauline, and got herself even more securely wedged in preparation. The thought that she was a hardy soul and that the jerk of a drop would be felt less on an elastic nylon rope than with ordinary cordage gave me a good deal of comfort. I pushed and strained. Lowered a boot gingerly. Met a glazed surface. Withdrew it. Lowered the other boot, but fared no better. There was nothing for it but to trust to luck and take radical measures.

I put down my left hand to a much lower hold. Slithered, barked a knee, and finished up trembling all over about a yard lower down. From there the descent to Pauline's stance was merely a matter of slow and careful movement.

Soon we were together again with the rope in a bit of a tangle, and no room for either of us to move. It may have been due to nervous reaction or too great a physical strain, but just at this moment I was seized with violent muscular cramps in the stomach and started writhing about (as much as circumstances permitted) in acute pain. For the first and only time that day Pauline looked anxious. The attack went on for some time, and when it was over the only word I could pronounce was "water." Pauline opened the water-bottle and I drank. She told me she was feeling sick herself and a little dizzy. Knowing her habit of under-statement I gathered it must be pretty bad. "Ha! ha! what a couple we are," I said. "The one with cramp, and the other with mountain-sickness."

I was somewhat weakened and feeling sick myself, so it was impossible to start down for some time. Eventually we pulled ourselves together and began.

But nearly an hour had passed since we entered the couloir. The short day had by this time faded, and we saw with keen disquiet that the rocks had withdrawn into menacing, tone-less shade. The sky looked bleak and steely, and there was nowhere to sit or lie or sleep. All was curving and sloping relentlessly downwards. The roof-tile slabs and the frown-ing pinnacles, the ice-filled cracks and the leering walls, seemed congregated round to encompass our destruction.

Down. The operative word was "Down." And swiftly, too. Pauline rose splendidly to the occasion and descended a full rope-length without a pause, confident she would be held whatever she did. I followed with extreme care and caution till we rejoined. Then I saw it: the snow-ledge. To our left, about sixty feet below, was a snow-ledge just under a short vertical block of rock that would protect it from anything that might fall. "That's the place," I thought, but said nothing to Pauline. We descended another rope-length and I strode triumphantly on to the ledge with the self-satisfied smile of a conjurer who has produced a rabbit out of a hat.

" What, that ? " she said. " But how can we ? "

It is true that the snow-ledge did not seem to have any foundation of rock below it : also that it sloped outwards and downwards. But I saw a texture of such firmness that there seemed little risk. " Come on, girl, do some work." I took off the rucksack, grabbed my axe with gloved hands, and started levelling off a platform with the wildest energy. Pauline soon followed suit, kicking with her boots, and after ten minutes of strenuous effort, which sent the blood tingling through us, we had created a more or less level place about two feet wide and perhaps nine feet long.

Pauline took off her duffel coat and laid it down. Where it ended I placed on the snow a big piece of white felt and then a down sleeping-bag and a kapok one. " For you. Take off your boots and hop in while you are warm." She lost no time in getting into the down bag fully clothed and wearing four pairs of socks. Then we pulled on the kapok one. On top of that I provided her with a woollen helmet and a nylon tent-sack about four feet long.

After that, it was my turn. I got into the other down bag, but found my climbing-breeches so wet from sitting on snow that I decided to take them off. So I stood up and proceeded to do this. Pauline's head emerged from the tent-sack. " Hey, what's happening ? You too hot or something ? " My breeches descended to reveal a pair of blue woollen bathing-trunks (which I always like to wear on such expeditions), and the sight was too much for Pauline. She subsided into helpless laughter ; then sighed for a little daylight to enable her to get her Contax to work.

I put on several pullovers and sweaters, plus a balaclava helmet, and on top of them my Grenfell jacket with hood.

The sleeping-bag felt cold and my bare knees and thighs were shivering.

Darkness had fallen, and above our heads the stars blazed.

We were too sick and tired to eat. I made some tea with a tommy cooker, and the hot liquid brought comfort to our insides. But before I had managed to finish mine it had turned to solid ice.

The time was 6.15 P.M. and we laid ourselves down for the night. Pauline had the inner berth. We were feet to feet, and my legs were on the outside, one foot over the edge. As the ledge was only about nine feet long, we overlapped slightly.

Even after a comparatively short passage of time the memory of that night has become blurred. But the thing which stands out most sharply is a vision of stars—stars blazing in that clear planetary air with an effulgence that is altogether impossible to communicate to anyone who has not witnessed it. We seemed to belong more to the skies than to the rocks and snow that cradled us. And sometimes I had a disembodied feeling almost as if we were floating in the great spaces themselves.

My thighs and knees became colder and colder and I suffered much discomfort. The air was so bitter it hurt to breathe, and when one put one's head inside the sleeping-bag the condensation of breath was so great that everything dripped. It was impossible to think of sleeping, because I might have turned and rolled over the edge. Pauline slept on and off and said she was quite comfortable, but I hardly believe it.

Every now and then we would ask each other what we thought the time was, and always guessed it too early so as not to be disappointed when we looked at our watches.

The hours came and went.

I saw clouds beginning to pile over the western Taurus peaks. And from time to time a faint sigh of wind moaned gently among the rocks above us. It was an eerie feeling.

Finally, after what seemed an unending succession of slowly turning hours, the first pallor of day began to show in the sky; the glaze of stars withdrew from a vivid present into the beginnings of a retrospect which could never again recapture the proximity of that revelation. But I have never greeted a dawn with greater enthusiasm.

The light grew stronger and stronger. Soon we could discern the Gürgün Su and details of the valley below us.

The snowy dome of the Argeaus took on a first crimson blush of sunlight, and we saw a vague black cone sticking up in the sky against the clouds perhaps eighty miles to the west of us. The cone got sharper in outline and descended. Then it touched the land and crept lower down. It was a long time before we realised that what we had seen projected in the skies was the shadow of the DK—an aerial image of the great mountain near whose summit we had so precariously lain.

I made tea with the last tommy cooker and we ate a little food. Everything was frozen hard, and my camera shutter refused to work. I dropped the tommy cooker over the edge and we heard it tinkling and clanging for minutes on end— down, down, down, growing fainter and fainter, but still moving.

Then there was a sudden whizz, and a stone flew past our heads on a note that indicated a high velocity.

108

On the Demirkazik

Getting the boots on was a real effort. They were as hard as boards, and needed minutes of massage. The seat of my breeches was crackling with ice, and until I managed to thaw it, highly fragile. We packed the sleeping-bags and roped up.

"Down," I said.

"Wouldn't you like to continue?" asked Pauline. But I thought this would be unwise. We were too weakened from lack of food and sleep, and it was useless taking chances with the weather, which did not now give the same promise as the day before.

We started the descent. First of all on glazed slabs and icy ribs, moving one at a time with great care; then on easier rocks, and finally on comfortable ground where we unroped and wandered slowly downwards, resting at intervals on the way to give Pauline's mountain sickness a chance. The sun finally reached us and we basked with gratitude in its rays, conscious more than ever before in our lives of the gift of that light which one so often takes for granted.

Before midday we were down on *terra firma*. Neshet and the little boy tended to our wants, and we ate a fuller meal than we had done for some time.

As we reclined on the warm earth afterwards, we looked back to our adventures among the high rocks, and though I regretted the failure of our enterprise Pauline seemed happy that we had achieved what we did. Her taste in such trips inclines to the ill-planned and the reckless; the more haphazard an expedition, the better she likes it!

After a good rest we set off back to Chukur Bağ, riding our donkeys into the afternoon sun over the slopes and ridges; and as the shades of evening drew on, we saw ahead the poplar trees whose shimmering leaves had framed the DK on the morning of the day before.

Our friends at the village greeted us with great warmth. They were happy to see us back alive, and not a little in awe of our having survived a night at such a height.

Mustafa Güler invited us to take dinner in his house. Neshet and Abdullah and several other villagers also came, and a huge peppery stew of beans, with occasional rare lumps of meat, was placed on the fire.

Before dinner the men took it in turns to say their prayers on a prayer-mat that was brought into the house for this purpose. They reversed their caps so that the brim was on the neck and knelt down and touched the ground with their foreheads several times, as well as reciting prayers standing up before the mat. All this took place with a complete absence of self-consciousness and amongst animated general discussion. Our friend Mustafa was not above interrupting one of his prayers to make a telling point in the conversation. All he did was to change the tone of his voice to say it.

We were asked if we would be well paid for our climb, and how much " They " would give us. When I demurred, Abdullah said, " Well, I suppose all you will get then is a straight payment on a kilometre basis for the journey." They could not understand we were travelling for pleasure and on holiday. In fact, the meaning of the word " Holiday " did not seem to be comprehended.

About half-past seven the stew was cooked and we all dipped in. The villagers used flaps of the wafer bread to eat with, but as a special concession we were given wooden spoons.

After dinner Pauline was invited to the " Haremlik," or

women's quarters, whither she was dragged by a shy young girl who was all giggles and embarrassment. There she was made to sit on a throne of cushions and had to produce full information about her underclothes. Her relationship with me called for a lot of explaining. They found it difficult to understand how any girl could be allowed to go about alone and talk to men—much less travel with one. Pauline had to explain that, in her country, it meant nothing and that she and I were ordinary companions in the same way as one man could be the friend of another.

Meanwhile I was trying to make polite conversation with our host and inquiring after his crops. He replied that this was a matter which was hardly of interest to him yet. " You see," he added, " I have been away for fourteen years. I lay in prison, and only came out with the recent amnesty." I swallowed twice on hearing this and inquired how such a sad fate had come to afflict him. He merely said, with an odd glint in his eye, " Oh, there was a very big accident at that time." Connecting this with his remarks about being a widower for fourteen years, I shuddered. And worse was to follow. When Pauline returned, he suggested carrying his duties as a host so far as to sleep with us that night.

This was really too much and I put my foot down. " In any case," I said, " the lady official and I are worn out and we'd like to have a bath if this is possible."

A cauldron was placed on the fire, and our hosts finally left us with a small tallow lamp. The water got piping hot and we did actually have baths—of a sort. At the far end of the room was a raised semicircular platform of dried earth with a high rim, sloping down to a small escape hole. And by taking turns, with the light extinguished, we got a complete wash in really hot water. It was an exquisite luxury.

To enjoy to the full the comfort of sleeping on a soft mattress in a warm room, it is necessary only to bivouac the night before in about 25° of frost on a ledge eleven thousand feet up on a rock-face. I can recommend this method to every reader. We ourselves found it extraordinarily efficacious, and were soon wrapped in the most glorious of slumbers.

The morrow saw us saying a regretful farewell to the assembled villagers from whose hands we had received such uncalculating hospitality. They refused all offers of money, though we paid Neshet quite a sum for his donkeys, and distributed a few small gifts.

As a valedictory gesture, Mustafa informed us with great pride that he was marrying again on the following Sunday— a sixteen-year-old maiden.

CHAPTER VII

JOURNEY TO HIERAPOLIS

SINCE January 1946, when I embarked on a business career, commercial travels have taken me over large parts of Turkey. I have slept in ditches, been snowbound in the car, overcome by landslides and even been dragged out of mud by a tractor. On one occasion two representatives of our English principals, who wished to see all the Turkish market in a week, had me as guide on a frantic journey by taxi. We were on the go for seventeen to twenty-one hours a day; in ten days we covered over two thousand three hundred miles along shocking roads, as well as doing a daily stint of five or six hours' sales-work. But I would not wish to enlarge on such lunacy.

Of all the voyages I have undertaken, there is one that stands out happily in memory as having the most interesting and amusing incidents, and my notes on it are sufficiently full for an account to be given.

Most of my business travelling involving long sales or market tours has been by taxi. With trains only two or three times a week to some places, and bus services very primitive, a car is the only way of covering a lot of ground quickly. And experience proves that it is far cheaper in Turkey to use taxis than to run a private car. The local taxis are powerful, heavy American automobiles, which are the only vehicles capable of standing up to the rough roads and giving any comfort to the passenger.

The Turkish taxi-driver is an interesting type of man to meet. Some members of the profession have nothing to learn when it comes to rapacity or crookedness—" straight as a corkscrew," in the words of a friend of mine—but nearly all are spirited and adventurous; and occasionally one meets a man who combines boldness with honesty, and a loyalty to his employer which is sometimes pushed to extremes involving a sublime disregard for the car. I know one such driver in Istanbul who has become a real friend.

In the journey to be described, I had flown down to Smyrna one autumn evening for the purpose of doing a market research and sales trip along all the towns in the Mæander Valley. This involved visiting as many centres and villages as possible, and practically every shop or booth. Our head salesman, Vassili, was already in Smyrna and awaiting instructions. It only remained to find a good man to take us.

I enlisted the aid of my cousin, R. E. Wilkinson. Besides being British Consul in Smyrna, R. E. W. is one of the world's leading authorities on the Hellenistic remains of Asia Minor, and a mine of information on almost every other subject to do with his parish.

We sat taking tea out-of-doors that afternoon in Bournabat. The great gardens, with their cypresses, and the ancient homes around us slumbered in the dreamful repose of a November day; the air had that golden quality of gentleness and warmth which makes the autumn in Smyrna so fair a season.

" What about the car ? " I asked. " Do you know a

reliable man ? Resolute, and with a sense of humour. Of course he must be a good driver, and we can't afford more than thirty *kurus* a kilometre."

My cousin pondered a little, and then replied : " Ahmet's your man. Just the chap. He's got a big black Dodge. High clearance, thirty horse-power. And it's the only taxi that has done any long-distance work in the Interior. I'll ring up the fellows at the Square and ask them to send him along to you this evening." And he went off into the house to crank up the telephone.

After dinner that night Ahmet arrived. He was a power-fully built, swarthy type of man, with laughing eyes and a long face. " I have never been so far into the Interior before," he said. " And the roads . . . who knows ? But if Allah gives permission and with the help of my thirty horses " (patting the bonnet of his car) " I will take you there."

We soon made a bargain, and after inquiring tenderly about the state of his tyres and other vital parts, I told him to collect Vassili the salesman, and pick me up at 6.30 the next morning. As the shops stay open about thirteen hours a day we had planned to be either travelling or out on our rounds throughout these hours. I intended to see most of the Mæander Valley, then climb on to the Anatolian plateau and visit Isparta, where the rugs come from, Burdur which is a provincial capital, and the beautiful lake town of Eğridir. Man proposes but Allah disposes : we could not foresee the many impediments in our way.

It was a radiant morning when we started from Smyrna. The waters of the Gulf danced in the early light, and the mountains looked unusually clear and blue against a pale sky. Vassili was ensconced cheerfully in the back amid a pile of wares and advertising material, while I sat with Ahmet in the front. We left Smyrna and took the road southwards towards Ephesus. It was a good road. The only good road. And Ahmet thought as much. " Vallahi," he laughed, " I am going to press it." And press he did. " It " being the accelerator, we were soon crashing along at eighty miles an hour. In almost no time we had reached Tepeköy, the first place on our list, and jumped out, ready to join battle or drink coffees with the local shopkeepers.

A little farther on was Selçuk, near the ruins of Ephesus. Ephesus was once a port, and a couple of thousand years ago ships used to call there ; but the waters have now far receded and the lesser Mæander has silted up. Of the prodigious temples and mighty architecture of the ancient town little remains but the columns and pediments, and the profusion of graceful marble which offer their forms to the eye of the tourist, set against the background of soft trees and hillside.

I wanted to see the ruins, but time was not our own, and we left Ephesus for another occasion. After Selçuk the road was less good. We picked our way onwards through a marshy valley imprisoned by abrupt and rocky hills. Numerous camels, untended and somehow forlorn, stood grazing or chewing in silence with an air of supercilious unconcern.

Soon we came to the Ægean Sea, and the wine-dark waters where the Ephesians of old sailed their ships. The coast was astonishingly varied and beautiful. Pine-clad slopes and steep crags, with coves of intensely blue water in between, alternated with stretches of sandy beach where the track often lay within two or three feet of the water's edge. Just out to sea were the clear-cut lines of the island of Samos, and away in the pearly northern distance I could make out the peaks of Chios.

We passed the fishing village of Kusadasi. And then, as the lights of evening began to twinkle from the houses, we came down the hairpin bends to Soke. This is a place which has suddenly sprung into wealth as a result of the cotton boom. There was good evidence of the fact in the grocery shops, where we saw phenomenal quantities of Turkish Monopoly liquor. It is said that more hard drink *per capita* is now consumed in Soke than anywhere else in the country. And sounds of revelry from the coffee-houses made me think that the name of the town was not inappropriate.

It had been dark for some hours when we left Soke and turned inland up the main Mæander Valley in the direction of Aydin. The night was warm and a great moon hung heavily over the lush plains, glinting silver on the occasional bands of mist. It was so bright that we hardly needed headlights. I remember passing through the dim ruins of Magnesia ab Mæanderum—the road almost brushes the temple of Artemis—and thinking of the wealth of ancient remains all round us. For it is in this region that the largest theatre in the world, some of the greatest temples, as well as the most perfect example of a Hellenistic city in existence, lie congregated within a few miles of one another. Many people know of Pergamum and Ephesus, but who has heard of Miletus, Prienae and Didyma, much less been there ?

We forded a couple of small rivers and bumped on steadily towards Aydin. Endless streams of camels made their deliberate, unhurried way past us, led by men riding diminutive donkeys. The camels were loaded with bulging sacks, from which an occasional white gleam at the broken edge revealed the presence of cotton ; and clinging to them like a veil, muffling their approach or their recession into distance, was a veil of moon-spangled dust. The leading animals had bells which shone in the moonlight and clanged with a slow, musical rhythm. These ghostly caravans riding through the night were the last survivors of a remote era, and soon destined to fade away before the tractor and the lorry. It gave one a strange romantic feeling to drive past them along that deserted plain.

Our arrival at Aydin, which is a large and prosperous centre, had the misfortune to coincide with the eve of market day, and the most exhaustive search of the available hotels and sleeping-places failed to reveal a bed. "We sleep out, then," I told Ahmet. He was shocked at the suggestion. "You will become ill, sir. Besides, it is most incorrect for a business gentleman like yourself to do that sort of thing." Vassili gave a snigger from the back. He was used to such imprudences.

We drove a couple of miles out of the town, and then backed up a small lane. The moon still shone, but the sky was dappled with swiftly moving clouds, now light, now dim ; and they seemed to be swinging up from the south.

I left Vassili in the back of the car and Ahmet in the front, and repaired to a nearby field. Under the silver leaves of an olive tree I got into a sleeping-bag and was soon being lulled to rest by the trill of night crickets and the tinkle of camel bells in the distance. Far away on the hills the call of a jackal added a disturbingly exotic note. It had been a very long day, but the multiplicity of impressions chasing round my brain tended to drive away sleep. And the luminous, moving sky gave a vague sense of unease.

At dawn on the morrow I found myself soaked with dew. Across the orange light welling up from the east, thin fringes of rain were falling gently from the clouds, and the chill of a November morning was in the air. I donned my brown suit (it was a nuisance to have to look presentable all the time) and knocked up Vassili and the driver. The windows of the car were thickly misted over and I could not see inside : it was evident that they were in no two minds about the dangers of " *le courant d'air.*"

We drove into Aydin again about half-past six, feeling distinctly like breakfast. Outside one of the coffee-houses an aproned assistant was shouting at the top of his lungs, " It's boiling, boiling hard, boiling ! " The announcement left us in no doubt that we were in front of the right shop. Breakfast in Anatolia is much the same wherever you go. You enter the coffee-house and see rows of stern-faced men, often heavily moustached and wearing coarse black breeches or leggings, grouped round the charcoal brazier in the middle of the room. On the brazier lies a great cauldron of milk, boiling furiously indeed. The master of ceremonies ladles it out into glasses which have previously received five or six spoonfuls of sugar, and a small boy with a towel over his shoulder scrambles nimbly round the patrons, ferrying steaming glasses of the concoction, or bringing back empties for a second helping.

On this morning, as usual, I asked for *Sadé,* or sugarless milk, and the request was received with the kind of raised eyebrow and pained expression a London hostess might direct at one of her guests who had committed some grave social solecism. But we reinstated ourselves by ordering three lots of bread and honey and clotted cream, which clearly showed we were out to cut a dash. It was a good, healthy breakfast and in keeping with the biblical ideal. By seven o'clock we were hard at work.

Aydin detained us some hours. It was a big place and contained over twenty thousand inhabitants, so we could not leave until nearly midday. The weather was now rather stormy and heavy rains were falling on the mountains to the north, though none had actually come down in Aydin. Ahmet showed doubts about the road. " From here onwards, sir, the way is not upholstered. It is in fact earth. And there are no bridges over the torrents." I had heard as much in Smyrna, but our job was just to press on.

The first few miles were tolerably good, though we had to ford two streams and plough our way through a great deal of light mud. Ahmet was always wanting to strike off on enticing side-tracks, and viewed with suspicion my authoritative pronouncements from the map. This was a new and dearly prized possession, for it was only in the last year that the Turkish Government had permitted the issue and sale of the twelve miles to the inch (actually 1 : 800,000) map. To be caught with one in the past was to risk landing up in a police station. But Ahmet was hardly up to these new-fangled ideas, and preferred to stop the car in front of every peasant who met us on the road and ask if we were on the right track. He had an astonishing variety of forms of address and I never ceased marvelling at the titles he fitted so aptly to each interlocutor and occasion. Sometimes it was " Brother," sometimes " Friend " or " Comrade," occasionally, to men of more authoritative mien, it was

" Sergeant " or " Father," and once when we met a woman he called her " Auntie " with perfect success.

The sudden appearance of a lorry from whose driver Ahmet wanted information about the state of the road ahead posed a new problem in etiquette, and I waited in suspense to hear how he would deal with it. The driver was an elderly man with leathery, dark-brown features, and he wore a white skull-cap. Ahmet took his measure in a trice, and began with a " *Merhaba, Kamyonju Ağabey* "—" Good day, elder brother lorryman." They were soon conversing volubly and I gathered from the *Kamyonju Ağabey* that we were in for trouble. His last words in fact were, " You can never get through."

Ahmet frowned, then gave two short blasts on his horn, and the lorry-driver replied with a couple of toots as he rumbled off. " A good, educated man," remarked Ahmet approvingly. " But it is sad to see how badly brought up the younger generation is now. Only last week I stopped on a hill to let a man go past me. And do you think he tooted ? Not even once ! " Among chauffeurs in Turkey there is a certain code of courtesy, especially outside the towns, and the unwritten laws of tooting are almost as complicated as the forms of marine salute and right of way. The rarity of other vehicles and the struggle against nature and bad roads make for a fellow-feeling between professional drivers that you will scarcely find in other places.

The parting words of the lorry-driver were soon to find confirmation. As we went along, the road became more and more sticky, and finally great pools of water and red mud showed that rain had preceded our coming. It was no longer possible to drive in top gear. We crawled along painfully in bottom, and as the hours went by I began to glance anxiously at the petrol gauge. Our track lay between tall banks surmounted by bamboo plants, which gave one a closed-in feeling. I was horrified on coming round one corner to see a veritable lake of mud ahead. There was no escape. Ahmet slithered the Dodge to a stop—the slightest pressure on the brakes caused a skid—and looked at the obstacle with a wary eye. "What do you think, sir?" "I should say we'll stick," I replied. "There is only one way," said Ahmet, "and that is to gather speed and rush it." Such aggressive spirit was admirable, but I felt alarmed at the possibility of a submerged rock or stone holing our sump in the process. So the worthy Ahmet got off his shoes and socks and waded into the red morass to take precautionary soundings. In places he was almost up to his knees.

After Ahmet had cleaned himself we backed the car and then charged into the semi-liquid lake. At first the momentum bore us bravely on, and a red tide of splashes came over the windscreen and bonnet, but then we sagged gradually to a halt, with the back wheels revving madly round. "Here we go," I thought to myself, "miles from anywhere, not a soul in sight, and stuck for the day." But Ahmet was equal to the occasion; before we had completely stopped, he made a lightning reverse, wrenched round his wheel, and presently had the car moving forwards again on a slightly different course. We just managed to suck ourselves out of the mud.

I had hardly recovered from the nervous strain of this episode when we were confronted by a new obstacle. It was a torrent-bed across the road which the recent rains had enlarged and deepened. A small stream was flowing angrily at the bottom of it and a liberal supply of stones and boulders gave a picturesquely life-like appearance to this slice of nature. The tracks of the lorry showed that it had come through, but it was obvious that our own clearance was not sufficiently high to pass the place. I gave vent to my feelings in florid language, but Ahmet was cheerfulness personified and chided me for displaying impatience. " It is the work of Allah, only He has power to do these things, and there is nothing we can do to alter His acts " ; then he turned to Vassili at the back who had sat in silence throughout, and said, " Sing, my little crow, why don't we hear your voice too ? " We all began laughing at that, and then got out and started heaving stones. In a quarter of an hour we had filled up the deepest trough, and lowered the height of some of the bumps to give a difference of height which the Dodge could clear. Vassili and I stood by while Ahmet drove her gingerly across.

Our petrol was now almost exhausted, and for once Ahmet was disposed to consult me as to the whereabouts of the next village or town. We had not far to go, but on arrival we found that there was no petrol station. The only available petrol, so they told us, was in some barrels near a disused stable at the eastern end of the village. " Very good," remarked Ahmet, " let's go, then." But I suddenly discovered I was hungry, so we sat down and consumed a bottle of wine and some bread and cheese—the first food for many hours—before going off to the stable. Ahmet got up rubbing his stomach, and after a few propitiatory gurks went over to the Dodge and ran his hand in a lovingly paternal manner over her mud-bespattered bonnet: " Well, well, we have generously filled our bellies and must now fill hers, otherwise she won't take us any farther." This was easier said than done. The barrels near the stable had rusty tops, and it was difficult to get them off. When we did succeed in doing it the fuel had to be siphoned off into our tank with a rubber tube. Ahmet was forced to get his mouth full of petrol in the process. " Ah, how it has destroyed the taste of that wine ! " he sighed. We filled up the tank and, using what appeared to be an extremely haphazard calculation, Ahmet paid a loafing bystander who seemed to be in charge.

The day was already far spent, but many miles remained before we could reach the haven of Nazilli town. I was already dreaming of the pleasures of a bed, and possibly even sheets, but the question was, would we get through ? On the mountains to our left a mass of slate-coloured clouds was discharging its contents with baleful assiduity, and the outlook was far from certain. We negotiated several further stretches of appalling mud, and crossed a number of torrent-beds. It was slow, exasperating work, but Ahmet's heart never faltered. His nerve and skill filled me with admiration, and he treated each new obstacle as a joke.

Just as dusk was falling we came to a particularly bad stretch where the road skirted the flank of a hill and was surmounted by a steep bank. Part of the bank had given way, and below it was a glutinous bog, effectively barring further progress. Suddenly a rock rolled down the bank and landed in the quagmire with a sickening plop that sent the mud flying. We looked up and saw, balanced on the slope, an elderly bearded gentleman, assisted by a youth, both wielding picks. Ahmet showed little surprise at this astonishing sight, and shouted up, " May God give you strength, father." The old man replied with a polite greeting, and explained that he and the youth were passengers in a lorry which had been forced to a standstill just round the next corner; they were evidently hoping to improve the condition of the road by their labours, for large stones and pieces of rock continued to descend the hillside with alarming impetus and frequency. I suggested to Ahmet that he should back away slightly, and we stopped to watch. The highway finally presented the appearance of a morass filled with partially submerged hard objects. Ahmet gazed reflectively at the scene and remarked, " Why, it's almost an upholstered road they've turned it into." He used the word to mean " metalled," and I could not help feeling that this was a somewhat optimistic euphemism.

The next step was to fill up the spaces with brushwood and branches, and by the time it was dark the work of correcting this temporary deterioration of the surface had been completed. The old man and the boy returned to the lorry —whose driver had apparently not even deigned to set foot on the ground—and we saw the glare of headlights coming round the corner. " Let him pass," I said to Ahmet, who waited to see what would happen. The lorry crunched and ground its way over the bad place, while disturbing thuds and crashes told us that the rocks underfoot were by no means immobile. Vassili and I got out and let Ahmet run the Dodge across in the tracks the lorry had made for us. Just then a heavy shower of rain started.

We continued our way through mud and rain until I saw a faint glow in the distance which we deduced was Nazilli. Vassili gave a cheer from the back, and Ahmet remarked, " Even our little crow is singing now." But hardly were the words out of his mouth when the headlights were extinguished. Ahmet gave a curse. It was the first and only time I saw him perturbed. He dived for his bag of implements and started tinkering about. But there was nothing to be done. Tinker and toil as he would, the current obstinately refused to run to our lights. We pulled wires, lifted the bonnet and ran the torch over all sorts of unlikely parts of the engine. After an hour and a half I told Ahmet he would have to drive on without lights. I did not fancy another night in the open.

We sat still for a few minutes in the dark; then, his eyes more attuned to the obscurity, Ahmet let in the clutch and started off cautiously. The clouds were luminous and moon-blanched: a vague light filtered through from the sky. We drove gropingly on, cheered by the ever-closer vision of lights ahead, which soon became so bright as to make it difficult to see the road. The nearest light of the town was only a few hundred yards off and I was already thinking of bed, when an ominous roar smote our ears. "Careful, Ahmet; what's that?" He drove on more slowly without a word. Suddenly, I felt the car slip and noticed we were in a few inches of water. Then through the trees just ahead we saw it. A roaring torrent, fully twenty feet wide, coming down with such force that boulders were thundering and grinding against each other in their flight along its bed. "*Paidos*," I said to Ahmet, meaning, roughly, "We've had it." On the other side of the torrent we could dimly make out a bus and two village carts.

It was apparent that a cloudburst had occurred on the mountains to our left. No vehicle or human being would be able to cross those raging waters now. Ahmet showed a

126

mild disappointment, but nothing more. His temperament was evidently well-adjusted to the uncertainties of local travel.

We saw headlights to our rear, and a few minutes later a jeep with two Turkish army officers and a military driver had drawn up behind. Their headlights flashed on to the foaming red waters in front of us, and over the two carts and the bus. One could now see that the brightly painted bus was crammed full of passengers—a sea of white faces stared at the torrent from behind the windows. The coach-work was decorated with floral motifs. In front, above the driver, was a motto in large letters : " ALLAHA EMANET," and underneath, in smaller ones, appeared the words " Güle Güle." Loosely translated these phrases mean, " IN THE HANDS OF GOD," and " Keep smiling." It was a good motto for a bus in these parts, and most appropriate to the circumstances.

After we had waited for some time Ahmet opened a box containing large quantities of oily cotton-waste and string, and I watched with interest as he proceeded to open the bonnet of the Dodge and wrap up sundry parts of the engine in swaddling bands of cotton-waste, burning his fingers in the process. " So that we can cross as soon as possible," explained Ahmet. " Have you gone crazy ? " I replied. " Not with me in the car, you don't ! " " But the torrent will soon go down ; it's not raining any more."

Ahmet was right. In less than an hour the flow of water was much less, and the boulders had stopped rumbling along the bed of the stream. One of the cart-drivers began to get restive and we watched with bated breath as he forced his horse into the torrent. The wretched animal stumbled and nearly collapsed twice, but eventually emerged dripping on our side. The military were the next to make the attempt. Their jeep almost stuck about ten feet from the far bank, but in the end they succeeded in crossing. Ahmet would not wait a moment longer. He revved up his engine, and charged without lights into the torrent. I closed my eyes, hoping for the best. The waters sucked and gurgled round us, and I heard stones grinding under the wheels. Finally we were through. In hot pursuit of the jeep, we shot past " IN THE HANDS OF GOD " and " Keep smiling," inspired by the hope that the headlights of the military would guide us into Nazilli.

Five minutes later we drew up at the door of the hotel. Naturally, it was full. We tried a second hotel, but were likewise disappointed. After this I invoked the aid of the police, thinking privately of the local prison, but they rose to the occasion and led us to a low kind of sleeping establishment. Apparently this was the " Third hotel." A slatternly old crone wearing a yashmak met us at the door and said, " No beds," then changed her mind on seeing our companions and said, "Only two." Being used to hard bivouacs, I offered to sleep in my bag and let Vassili and Ahmet have the two beds. Ahmet would not hear of it, and said he could easily spend another night in his car. So we shook hands with him (the occasion seemed to demand it) and wished him good-night.

Our " hotel " was full of peasantry who were sleeping, fairly heavily dressed, in large brass bedsteads arranged in lines down the passages. The few rooms were crammed with similar beds, and a chorus of snores met us as we went up the stairs. On the upper passage a zinc basin with a tap above

128

it supplied the only washing facilities; the toilet consisted of a draughty chamber with a hole in the floor, served by an entrance which had a transparent pane of glass only five feet or so above the floorboards.

As we went to bed an elderly bearded peasant started complaining that he was incommoded by the smell emanating from a sack under his neighbour's bedstead, to the point where he could not sleep. The creature who had originally opened the door to us came up to investigate, and after applying her nostrils to the sack, announced in a loud voice to all and sundry, " It is only grain—now go to sleep, father, and stop worrying. What will these foreigners think if you complain ? "

Vassili appeared embarrassed by such unusual surroundings, but I was so tired I curled up on the bed in my bag and was soon asleep.

II

We spent some time in Nazilli and did work in the surrounding places. I judged it only prudent to defer our departure for Denizli—the last town in the Mæander Valley and the most important—until the road had had a chance to dry off a bit. Besides her other troubles the Dodge had a badly dented sump and required all the attention the garages of Nazilli could lavish on her. As for Ahmet, he was in need of a rest.

When we started out for Denizli I realised that this would be the last lap of our outward journey. Lack of time now made it impossible to think of visiting Isparta, Burdur and Eğridir, but I consoled myself by reflecting that we would do an extra thorough job in Denizli, and perhaps have an hour or two to visit Hierapolis nearby. My cousin in Smyrna had told me on no account to miss seeing the place. "Certainly the most remarkable thing in Anatolia," he had said ; "and the view from the top of the petrified terraces has been described in old writings as the most beautiful in the world."

The sun shone and the mountains looked clean and near as we left Nazilli. It was a fair morning, with every colour standing out sharply in the cool air. Up on the hillsides the beeches glowed in autumn richness, and in the valley an occasional giant plane tree shivered its golden foliage in the breeze.

The road from Nazilli onwards was worse than anything we had yet experienced, but the conditions were somewhat drier. We had a lot of trouble with torrent-beds and stones, but less with mud. As we drove slowly eastwards the country-side began to look wilder. It still retained something of the graciousness of the Ægean littoral, with its feeling of cultivated softness, but you sensed at the same time that the sterner climate and landscapes of the plateau were approaching. By and by we passed some black tents on the hillside. "Yürük nomads," remarked Ahmet. "Instead of inhabiting a house they throw down tents. The Government cannot get any taxes from them, nor do they provide sons for the army." Having effectively damned the Yürüks he added as an afterthought, "When the police catch them they hold them for a long time and make them become soldiers."

Later on we overtook what appeared to be a group of these nomads. The road was narrow and hemmed in by steep banks. Ahmet became exasperated. Acts of God and nature had left him unperturbed. But to have his way blocked by Yürüks, that was something no self-respecting chauffeur could endure. The rear of the caravan was composed of wild-looking children, and women dressed in disturbingly vivid colours, accompanied by camels. The women were walking and the smaller children were swathed like mummies and strapped on to small pulpit-like erections fixed on the backs of the camels, just above their tails. Some of the camels were beautifully caparisoned and bore loads of heavy black material which looked like woven horse-hair. I took this to be the famous Yürük tenting. There were smaller adolescent camels with lighter loads, as well as a few baby camels which trotted along unhampered by any weight.

We slowly got past the camels and came up into the next department, which consisted of small boys driving donkeys. I was astounded to see that each donkey had a kind of built-up nest on its back, and that each nest contained a couple of hens, or a cock and a hen. The roosters seemed to be travelling in every comfort and made no attempt to leave their peripatetic thrones. But the sight of poultry riding on donkeys was somehow ridiculous, and even Ahmet forgot his vexation to laugh at it.

The donkeys were preceded by majestic flocks of sheep and goats in the charge of young men, and after we had got through the flocks we came to older men riding horses. In front, leading the whole caravan, was a lone hunched-up figure astride a splendid grey-and-white horse. He was some way ahead and I glanced at him curiously as we passed. He was an old man with a thin, pointed beard and a very brown wrinkled face, having something of the Tartar in its bone structure. A ruthless face, but one of great dignity. " The head of the tribe," was Ahmet's only comment.

Our onward journey to Denizli was not without incident; for we became bogged at a seemingly innocent place, and it took four hours' work to get us out. But by the evening of the same day I was thrilled to see the mighty mountain shapes of Cadmos and Salbakos (now the Honas Dağ and Baba Dağ) rising above the nearer hills. It was a sign that the end of our outward journey was approaching. As we drove into Denizli after dark the rustle of leaves and the clear sound of running water made me sense the unseen proximity of high mountains and forests. The air already had a trace of the sharpness and invigoration of keener climates.

Denizli is an enchanting place. When we woke up the next morning we saw trees shimmering in the morning light and masses of crystal-clear water running past the hotel. The town is built on the hillside and has a most picturesque old market-place, where antique booths nestle under plane trees, connected by cobbled alleys on different levels and surrounded by a wall. We spent all of one day hard at work, and the greater part of a second day. It was only towards the evening of the second day that I was satisfied we had done all we could. Vassili and Ahmet had their eyes on a tea-shop and were mentally savouring the delights of sticky cakes, when I announced brutally that there would be no tea-shop but a drive out to Hierapolis. The distance was fifteen miles, and with an hour to sunset I hoped there would be just time to see the famous petrified terraces and the ruins.

We drove from Denizli down into the Mæander Valley, passing through the ruined theatre and aqueduct of Laodicea, then crossed the Mæander and bore due north. In front of

132

us on the hills was a great blotch of white rather like snow. As we approached, it became possible to make out details, and we saw, gradually unfolding its secret before us, a great natural amphitheatre, perhaps four hundred feet high and half a mile round. The semicircular walls of the amphitheatre are composed of vertical pitches of white stalactites, arranged in beautiful curves and volutes, and towering up like so many fantastic collections of snowy organ-pipes. Below each battery of organ-pipes are small flat terraces with rims, like rounded gold-fish ponds, and below the terraces further curved and fluted sections of organ-pipes. The whole effect is rather like that of a frozen waterfall on the most majestic possible scale.

The road continued right up past the cliffs, and we bumped along on a kind of ramp of solid rock. Traces of Roman flagstones showed where an ancient carriageway had been imposed on the bed of rock. We climbed higher and higher and eventually emerged onto a small plateau above the level of the petrified terraces. All round were ruins, invisible from below, but here revealing the extent and opulence of the city which was once Hierapolis. Before us lay columns and tombs, lofty walls and a massively built temple. On the hillside at the back was a Roman theatre, almost perfectly preserved, with seats, I am told, for 10,000 spectators. To the left was an older Hellenistic theatre, dismembered by rains and the passage of the centuries, mouldering to rest on an eroded hillside. The whole scene was bathed in the orange light of a declining day, and the warm brown walls and columns seemed almost on fire with the richness of the colour.

The view across the plain was spacious and commanding.

133

Hierapolis : a general view of the terraces

Below us we could see the serpentine sweeps and whorls of the Mæander, fading away into the glowing west, and opposite, behind Denizli, Cadmos and Salbakos reared their amber-tinted snowy peaks to the sky. There was a great silence everywhere. Neither did anything move. We might have been looking on to a lost world, and for a moment I had the feeling that the forward-flowing stream of time had reversed its flow and was ebbing quietly back.

The camera at my side brought me back to earth, and after a quick tour of the horizon I scrambled down onto the terraces and took a series of hurried photographs of the frozen waterfalls and snowy organ-pipe formations within the circuit of the great amphitheatre. The rock seemed to be limestone. It was vividly white, and though trickles of liquid were oozing down, the footing was firm and handholds safe. At one place a cascade of warm water fell plunging from the plateau, and everything within reach of the spray was coated in fresh layers of white. Even the few rock plants nearby bore a glistening white calcareous shroud. They say that if you lower a basket into the waters it becomes petrified within the hour.

I followed the main stream up to its source on the plateau. The channel, instead of being cut into the land, was raised above the general level, and wound in and out of the walls and columns to a large pool with extremely clear blue-green depths. This was the site of the waters, and in their mysterious profundities you could see ancient columns and broken capitals, blocks of marble and Greek lettering. Bubbles oozed slowly upward; the water was welling in from below. Here was the secret of Hierapolis, the carver and creator of the petrified terraces, and the *raison d'être* of the town.

In the pre-Christian era the waters themselves were venerated, and the Plutonium nearby bears witness to the rites connected with the worship of the vapours from Pluto's Underworld. These rites are later said to have been adapted by the early Christians, who took over the Plutonium and used the temple for celebrating their own ceremonies connected with Holy Water. The waters of Hierapolis are warm—almost hot—and remain at the same temperature all the year round. At the start of their life in the pool they are pellucid and inviting. By the time they reach the valley below they have cooled and taken on the opacity and whiteness of milk.

I felt tempted to have a bathe, but already it was getting dark. Ahmet was restive about the road back and we were due to make a very early start on the morrow. So I returned slowly along the stream channel and watched the after-glow of sunset still flaming amid the high clouds. The snows of Cadmos and Salbakos had retired into a toneless steely pallor which showed up wanly against the deeper hue of the sky. And the Mæander Valley slumbered grey and formless below us. Shafts of mist, and a little smoke from a village, lay still upon the air. There was no movement and no life anywhere. With the fading light the universe seemed to have stopped.

Sometimes, when I look back to the hurried moments spent at Hierapolis, I feel the urge to return and see it at leisure. But this would be a mistake. The experience was unexpected and unforgettable. And the vividness of those first impressions must, in all probability, remain untouched.

135

CHAPTER VIII

SWITZERLAND REVISITED—THE GREAT PEAKS

THE summer after my journey to Hierapolis I had the opportunity to travel to the Alps again, and felt drawn once more to those Zermatt giants whose summits had provided such golden memories.

During the winter months, when Istanbul lay grey under the pall of Black Sea scud, and the mosques were whitened by the blizzards from Bulgaria, my mind went winging out, as the minds of mountaineers are wont to do, to the peaks of summer. And the two places which I thought of most were the angular crests of the Mischabel and the peerless and lovely Weisshorn. Beyond this I had the wish, almost kept secret from myself, to do that noble and classic traverse of the Matterhorn by the 'Zmutt and Italian Ridges, which is so steeped in legend and association, and where the strands of history, particularly on the Italian Ridge, are woven into almost every passage.

Mid-July saw me passing once again by the magic names of Stalden, St Niklaus, Randa and Täsch, and forsaking the thick air of the Rhone Valley for the serener atmosphere of the Mattervisp.

Miss Eberhardt and Mme. Casanova still ruled the Monte Rosa, and I was fortunate enough to have my familiar room. It was a pleasant arrival, for Alfons met me in the road, and we spent the first evening discussing our future expeditions with that happy detachment from considerations of weather which is the characteristic of mountain plans made in advance.

The sound of the goats with their bells being driven past the door, and the chimes of the church tower opposite, welcomed me home on that first evening with a sudden wealth of small memories that leapt up from their resting-place in the mind and suddenly joined the present to the past of two years ago.

Herr Alfred Zürcher was at the Monte Rosa ; it was an experience to meet this grizzled veteran of the hills whose legendary fame and outstanding exploits had spread over almost half a century of mountaineering. Zürcher was sixty-four then, but continuing to do arduous climbs. Only a year previously he was still being guided by Joseph Knubel, whose name was immortalised in G. W. Young's ' On High Hills.' Joseph Knubel, Zürcher, and Rudolf Lochmatter— a nephew, I believe, of the incomparable Franz—had climbed together as a famous trio for seventeen or eighteen years until this summer of '51, when an injury to Joseph's knee had forced him to give up guiding, and another of the Loch-matter family had stepped in to fill the breach.

I suppose Alfred Zürcher must be almost the last survivor of the grand tradition in mountaineering, when amateurs of ability and means climbed together with famous guides whom they engaged for season after season, to form a relation-ship altogether different from the present-day purely com-mercial dealings between amateur and guide. In the golden years the amateur formed a team with his guides, who were linked by name and reputation almost exclusively to their patron.

In the days of the Zürcher-Knubel-Lochmatter partnership, Lochmatter did the leading and step-cutting, looking only to himself and the way ahead. Knubel, as second on the rope, had as his main job to secure his employer. " A great guide and a real gentleman," said Zürcher. " He has been with me on two hundred and ninety 4,000-metre ascents. If it was not for his knee, he would be guiding me still."

I met Joseph Knubel, a thin, wiry man of unusual lightness. His hair was still reddish, and the features below alert and youthful, but quietly relaxed. On his face was written that mixture of serenity and strength which the greatest guides possess. Deeply religious, he never missed a Sunday service. Once when he and Zürcher had just finished up a twenty-three hour climb on the Grandes Jorasses (seventeen hours of it above four thousand metres) in the early hours of a Sunday morning, Knubel took only an hour's rest and then walked down to Chamonix to go to church.

Zürcher dresses simply in pale-brown tweeds and plus-fours. His manner is modest and quiet. In speech he is brisk, with a quaint interrogative " No ? " often placed at the end of his sentences. He looks rather like what Somerset Maugham must have looked fifteen years ago. And his features are burnt by fifty seasons of high glaciers and snow.

When in Zermatt he always puts in at the Monte Rosa. He told me with a twinkle in his eye that at the beginning of his life they used to give him a table at the far end of the dining-room. Now Mme. Casanova sees to it that he has the place of honour by the window on the street.

I asked if he had ever had an accident, and he said only one, a few years previously. This was on the Zinal Rothorn when a falling stone had grazed his head and cut a vein.

The blood came out so fast that it flooded the bandage. Then he clapped his shirt to his head and descended for five hours into Zermatt, with his hand pressing the shirt into place. They put nine stitches in, but two days later he was up the Matterhorn. And all this at the age of sixty.

One of the pleasantest references to Zürcher in climbing literature—of which I reminded him—comes in Smythe's account of the first ascent of the Brenva Face of Mont Blanc in 1927. After their tremendous struggles of thirty-six hours, broken only by a short, freezing bivouac, Graham Brown and Smythe reached the summit in a furious gale at 7.45 P.M. "Then somewhere in the dimness beneath, a minute spot of light flashed out. We were not forgotten. Herr Zürcher and his guides, Joseph Knubel and Graven, were waving a lantern. . . . That tiny speck of light, telling us that through many strenuous hours friends had watched us, was a happy inspiration indeed."

II

Alfons felt that we could not do better than make a start on the Riffelhorn again. And he proceeded to try me out on some impossible places, giving as an excuse, "You climb quite good now, so we do something a little difficult." The Glacier Couloir, the Outside Edge, and the Gackenloch all received our attentions, and I was then persuaded, much against my better judgment, to venture on a double-rope descent of a fifty-foot wall. My subsequent small experience of abseiling has in no way served to modify the initial feeling of revulsion which seizes me when forced to swing out over space to get into position. Once the descent has started and the body is in action, I feel no fear.

After putting me through my paces, Alfons hurried off on the 1.30 train from Rotenboden, *en route* for Zermatt and the Hörnli Hut. He had a customer for the Matterhorn on the following day. Sometimes guides will be working for days on end from 3 A.M. to 8 P.M., going almost non-stop from one high peak to another, via Zermatt. It is in this way only that they can make enough money in the brief and uncertain summer season to tide them over to the days of ski-instructing which occupy the winter months.

I wandered down to Zermatt from the Riffelhorn in a leisurely way, greeting as old acquaintances the line of peaks which towered across the valley. I looked with special care at the Zinal Rothorn, because Alfons was keen to take me on a difficult climb from the Rothorn Hut, over the Trifthorn and along the south ridge of the Rothorn. He described it in terms of such enthusiasm that I became won over to the idea, although after looking up the price of this expedition in the tariff, I decided it must be a *very* difficult climb.

Two days later we left Zermatt after lunch, carrying all our food and equipment for a couple of days in two fairly heavy rucksacks. Besides the Rothorn climb, I had decided to use the opportunity of finding ourselves at the Rothorn Hut for an ascent of the Obergabelhorn over the Wellenkuppe, with a descent by the Arbengrat.

It was a hot afternoon and the unending hairpins of the Trift path seemed more than usually wearisome. We arrived at the Trift Inn after a couple of hours, with dripping shirts. A short rest and cool drinks revived us for the next stage of the climb to higher regions. By and by we came up with

Hierapolis : petrified terraces

a thin, elderly gentleman of Eastern appearance, with white hair and a naked torso burnt a dark brown by the sun. He wore white celluloid-rimmed goggles and spoke perfect English. A pleasant conversation sprang up and we walked one behind the other on the long zigzags of the moraine leading up to the hut. He was climbing the Rothorn on the next day.

The Rothorn Hut is magnificently situated, nine thousand nine hundred feet up on a rock bastion under red cliffs, and it overlooks the glacier.

The air was bleak and thin when we arrived. We had a cold, remote view through rather misted atmosphere towards the vast snowfields of Monte Rosa, over the ribs and ridges of a high mountain world. The ordinary life of men and towns and fast-moving objects had vanished. Here only the ice-axe and the heavy boot, and the slow rhythm of mountain action could move one about. I felt that artificiality had ended; man was face to face with nature and the timeless, elemental forces.

In the hut people were already eating their supper when we arrived at 6.15. Great bowls of soup and eggs and spaghetti, cheese and fruit and wine, lay on the tables under the dim light. The shout of the hut-keeper as he pushed yet another vessel of steaming food through his hutch from the kitchen mingled with the clump of boots on wooden floors. The guides in toneful costume moved to and fro, each with his own chosen scheme of colour. Joseph Biner in red shirt and pale fawn breeches, the great Alexander Graven in his famous white peak cap, and Alfons in red lumber shirt, with light-brown breeches and a sash round his waist. It seemed to be a fairly experienced gathering of guides and amateurs. There was hearty eating and drinking. All our food was emptied into two baskets bearing the number of our mattresses, and we contributed a couple of cubes of Maggi soup to the general pot of fare. Then bed, upstairs.

The Rothorn Hut is a most modern establishment and built on quite a scale. The mattresses are sprung and laid one alongside the other, about fifteen or twenty in a row. You sleep within inches of your neighbour. There is a shelf for rucksacks and a rail for hanging clothes on. I took a sleeping-pill and fell asleep fairly soon.

I was already awake when the hut-keeper came in and lit the oil lamp about three in the morning. It was fine; the stars sparkled in the black sky. Sleepers groaned and stretched. Boots were put on. Soon everyone was down-stairs eating breakfast. Great jugs of melted snow-water— boiling hot—were being pushed through the hutch by the hut-keeper. With these you made your tea. Alfons got some eggs fried by privately monopolising one of the stoves, so that we had a satisfying meal.

After breakfast we roped up on the platform outside the hut. The sky was beginning to lighten, and a faint, greenish pallor showed already behind the Rimpfischorn, below a sickle-moon riding high above the peaks, with the old moon in its arms. We stepped on to the hard frozen snow of the glacier, which crunched exquisitely under our boots. The sensation of walking on the springy surface of a glacier in the early morning is hard to beat. The lantern casts its orange circle of light, the rope hangs from your left hand, the ice-axe in your right, and the rhythmical creak and crunch of snow marks the pace of progress to the uppermost world.

The Trift Glacier wafted us quickly heavenwards on this morning, and as dawn flooded the sky we stood near the foot of the ice couloir to the Triftjoch. I saw ahead on my right a great leaning wall of ridge towering up northwards. It had a livid hue in the cold, greenish light, and I found it quite impossible to judge its distance and dimensions. When Alfons said this was the ridge we should be engaged on later, I found it hard to believe the stories I had heard about the length of the climb, for it seemed hardly more than a couple of hundred yards in extension.

Alfons cut steps methodically up the ice couloir to the col. By the time we had reached the Triftjoch it was morning, with the sun just about to rise behind the Mischabel. It is always a good moment to reach a high pass, and I could hardly wait for Alfons's signal to come up the last few feet and see the other side. We looked down into the Zinal Valley, still slumbering in night, with shafts of mist veiling the lowest slopes; and on to the sudden revelation of a new world of mountains, valleys, glaciers, and peaks.

The Trifthorn is a ruin of grey slabs and thin edges, hung far above the glacier. Alfons began to swing up its crumbling rocks which exuded yet the cold of night. A short climb brought us to the summit and we stood there, at about 6 A.M., a couple of hours after leaving the hut. From here we could see a sweep of snow-ridge leading to farther rocks; then a crenellated edge of red spires, and pinnacles with frighteningly vertical drops on the right, which led up in a triumphant sweep to the summit of the Zinal Rothorn—our goal for the day.

It did not look far. Alfons said another six hours, and I made a mental reserve in favour of four. Actually we took

six and a half hours from the Trifthorn peak. The conditions were perfect. The sun shone brightly. The rocks
were dry. It was a privilege to be on the high ridges on
such a day, and the sweeping curves of snow from the Trifthorn bore us majestically downwards to the start of the
Rothorn Ridge. Alfons had warned me about cornices, and
when we left the snow and bore right I saw that the ridge
was hollow underneath, shaped like a wave about to curl
over and break.

We started on the Rothorn Ridge. The climbing was
very difficult, indeed rather beyond my standard at this
time. But the rock was grateful and warm to the touch,
and the magnificent red granite afforded holds that were
secure if sparse. We took all the gendarmes straight, and
I remember the variety of up and down climbing, the outcrops and pinnacles, the lurching towers and the craning
over space. One particular monster was thinner at its base
than it was on the summit, and in two places I just had to
rely on the rope. Alfons was in great spirits and urging me
on with laughter and encouraging remarks. We had the
ridge to ourselves and the whole day before us, so there
seemed no point in hurrying. I quickly revised my rash
estimate of the morning. The climb began to seem endless.
More than five hours must have elapsed before we got to
the Gabel or Fork of the Zinal Rothorn. Here we had lunch
and a good rest before assaulting the final rocks.

The route changes over here for a time to the Zinal side
of the mountain, where the famous Biner Platte is passed.
This is a smooth slab of considerable difficulty, especially
when descending. The nomenclature of most slabs or plattes
is rather macabre, being generally derived from the persons

who fell there. The Biner Platte on the Rothorn, like the Moseley Platte on the Matterhorn, is no exception.

The last problem on the Rothorn comes on the peak itself, when you have to traverse round a moving block. To do so it is necessary to lean the body out over space, above a precipice so smooth and so vertical that it must give a tremor to even the most hardened alpinist. If you dropped a stone there it would not hit anything for about three thousand feet.

We reached the summit at 12.30 after eight and a half hours on the ascent. The top of the Rothorn is a largish circular platform, isolated in space and comfortable to lie on. As a peak it cannot compare with the Matterhorn, but it is certainly more difficult to reach (by the Trifthorn Ridge). When we arrived, all the other climbers by the usual route had long since departed, and we lazed happily amid the high peaks in agreeable solitude, undisturbed by any jarring sound. In all directions, pale, creamy shades of mountain form stretched limitlessly around through the misty atmosphere. The rocks beneath us were warm. The air windless.

My fatigue made the descent painful. Alfons was bent on passing certain snow traverses and couloirs at a gallop, for fear of rock-falls. Actually, one volley of stones just missed him while he was crossing a couloir, and I had a demonstration of how fast he could move when under fire.

The snow was in shocking condition owing to the heat, and we were sinking in above our knees in some places. I fell down a number of times and got thoroughly wet. However, we were down in two and a half hours and I immediately retired to bed for a sleep, while Alfons wrestled with the drying of my breeches.

K   145

Snow cornices : the Trifthorn

There was a new crowd at the hut for dinner, and different sleeping companions. Two hearty Swiss matrons of a certain age were stationed to my left, and an unidentifiable blonde to the right ; next to her a guide called Kronig, with whom I had a sleepy conversation about the Young Ridge on the Breithorn before dropping off to sleep. It was a suspiciously warm night, and the constellations had a hooded look about them.

III

An early rising at 3 A.M. met with discouragement from the guides. The stars were obscured and gloomy, and the meteorological pundits who had ventured out on to the platform reported most of the sky as in cloud.

Breakfast was not served until 4.15. A lightening of the sky half an hour later encouraged some parties, including Alfons and myself, to set forth. But it seemed quite clear to me that the Obergabelhorn and the Arbengrat would not be ours that day. Strange cigar-shaped clouds lay poised above the summits, and the early morning snows had a pallid and unearthly wanness about them. To the south, over Italy, a wall of vapour was stemming up, with detached bastions of cloud trailing an added menace before it. I felt disappointed about the Obergabelhorn, but excited at the prospect of seeing the high mountains under conditions of storm. For contrasts are necessary to existence ; just as there can be no spring without winter, and no colour without its complement, so it is necessary to see the hills under all conditions in order to appreciate properly any single aspect of them.

There were four ropes of us ; three male parties bound, like Alfons and I, for the Arben Ridge, and one lady and her guide aiming only at the Wellenkuppe. Alfons led off at a relentless pace, but the snow on the glacier had barely frozen ; the crunchy, springy surface that had given a lilt to our steps on the day before, had changed into a crusted, spongy mass, where the boot broke through and sank in seven or eight inches at each step. I know of nothing more tiring than a long walk under these conditions. By the time we had reached the rocks at the base of the Wellenkuppe my muscles were aching, and I firmly called a halt. The two ropes of French students—very pleasant fellows—caught us up and passed us here. Then, in about ten minutes, we started climbing the rocks. After our struggles on the Rothorn Ridge I found these rocks very easy, and rushed up with great zest and enjoyment, stirred to faster action by the growls and claps of thunder on the Matterhorn. The great peak had now almost disappeared in vapour, and the grey shroud was reaching over the sky to where we were, overshadowing us with its threat.

Suddenly the rocks ended and we found ourselves on the final snowcap. At the same moment a few odd snowflakes came twisting down through the still air, out of the moving sky. The heavens went dark, and broken chips and rags of cloud came spinning across to us from the south. I looked up again and saw everything obscured around us, save the black prow of the Zinal Rothorn, standing out against vague patches of sunlight to the north, with the heavy grey pall already beginning to press on its top.

The snow got steeper and steeper until quite unexpectedly I found myself standing on the summit. As I did so, my ice-axe gave a nasty, hissing whine, and I dropped it on the spot. The French students' guide courteously picked it up, and I took it back, pretending somewhat dubiously that it had fallen by accident. My axe continued to whine and hiss, and I heard the other axes entering the choir. There were six of us congregated on the sharp ridge of the summit: Alfons and I, the guide with one French student, and a separate rope composed of the other two students alone.

When Alfons took his cap and hood off, his hair stood on end and I noticed a tingling in my own scalp. We were in the middle of an electrical field and the air itself seemed to prickle. Alfons said, "I think perhaps you puts the goggles on now." I was just about to slip them on, when there was a spark and a fairly strong electric shock travelled up my left arm. "No thank you," I replied. "They go back into my pocket." Meanwhile the desultory snowflakes fell, and the axes whined. I revelled in the strangeness of this experience and the stormy scene round us. The mountains had never looked more impressive than they did now, half hidden and half revealed, showing blackened and ominous summits, or livid and sinister ribs. "What about the Gabelhorn?" I asked. The French students smiled. Alfons gave a laugh. "You joke, I think. Now is the ridge very dangerous. We must immediately away."

As we turned to descend the Wellenkuppe snowcap a veritable blizzard began to fall. Then a flash of lightning blazed down so close that I seemed to feel the warmth of it. We were simultaneously enveloped in a muffled clap of thunder. Alfons and the students' guide increased their pace. We came quickly to the rocks, now rather more difficult to climb down in their condition of slitheriness, with

new snow constantly falling. In the haste and turmoil of our first flight from the dangerous ridge, it was some time before I could get my gloves on, and my hands became numb from clutching icy holds. The six of us, on three ropes, were clattering down with ice-axes jammed behind our rucksacks in a helter-skelter descent, linked by a comradely feeling which I imagine does not normally extend to separate ropes.

We reached the upper névé, and then started a racing kick-heel descent down the snowfield, over the glacier to the Rothorn Hut. People were drifting in through the clouds from other climbs, and none of the parties trying for the Rothorn had managed to reach their objective.

Alfons and I settled down to a hefty second breakfast, only four hours from our first; then we sat round for an hour chatting with the French climbers, who were a carefree and charming group. Their funds exhausted, they were going to travel back over the Triftjoch to Mountet and Zinal as soon as the weather cleared.

We left the Rothorn Hut at 9. I found myself feeling in the highest health and spirits in spite of the disappointment at missing the Arben Ridge. In friendly rivalry I raced Alfons down the five-thousand-foot descent to Zermatt, and by twenty past ten we pulled up, steaming, in front of the Monte Rosa Hotel, in the blander air of the valley. Apart from a few clouds in the upper sky, there was nothing to show that there had been any disturbance in the weather. The village diffused an air of peace and immunity to atmospheric commotions. The stout walls of the Monte Rosa offered protection from every vagary of climate, and the comforting presence of good furniture made me happily

" People were drifting in through the clouds. . . ."
(Wellenkuppe descent in storm)

aware of the benefits of returning to ordinary life. In the same way as I had felt a sense of liberation when reaching the withdrawal of the Rothorn Hut, so I appreciated the pleasure of reunion with the amenities of civilisation on my return.

IV

Alfons had noticed the flags flying at half-mast as we spun down the last hairpins from the Edelweiss Hotel into Zermatt. We thought immediately of some amateur climbing disaster, but while we were sitting outside the Monte Rosa the words " Otto Furrer, *gefallen am* Matterhorn " were brought to our ears. Alfons looked stunned ; he seemed unable to believe it. " Impossible," he murmured, " Otto was my best friend. A fine guide. And so very careful. He was more careful than I am myself."

The story makes very shocking reading. Otto Furrer was descending the Italian Ridge of the Matterhorn, and his customer, a lady climber, had just completed the descent of the " Tyndall Corde." This passage comprises a steep cliff, made negotiable by a long fixed rope, which is usually known as " La Grande Corde," although Zermatt guides call it the " Tyndall Corde," after Professor Tyndall. Although his client had used the fixed rope without mishap and reached safer ground, as soon as Otto Furrer started the descent the Tyndall Corde broke and he fell over a hundred feet. He was killed outright. Some lower projecting ledges and the climbing rope combined to arrest the fall of his body, but the lady climber was severely injured by the shock of his weight coming on her waist loop, and was dragged down some yards. A rescue party was formed and the lady climber was brought to safety. She later recovered completely in Brigue Hospital. It is curious to reflect that if the Tyndall Corde had broken under her instead of Otto Furrer, neither of them would have been injured and there would have been no accident at all. Otto Furrer's body was recovered and borne to Zermatt.

A good deal of ill-feeling was caused by this accident, which the inhabitants of the Valais ascribed to criminal negligence on the part of the Italian authorities. On the Swiss side of the mountain the fixed ropes are rigorously tested every year and renewed when necessary. No Swiss fixed rope has yet been known to break on the Matterhorn, and I believe this was the first time any of the Italian ropes had given way. For a guide to be killed on a standard route such as this was almost unheard of.

More than ninety-nine guides in a hundred die in their beds, and if one considers the hundreds or maybe thousands of ascents which each guide makes in a lifetime, it is easy to see that the chances of being killed with a guide on an ordinary route are so small as to be negligible.

Climbers get killed regularly every summer in Switzerland; from the nine or twelve thousand personal ascents likely to be made each season in Zermatt at least three or four are likely to end in tragedy. Almost always the tragedy comes to parties of guideless amateurs who have embarked on something beyond their skill and experience, or been surprised by adverse weather conditions. Greater mountaineering in the Alps demands a long apprenticeship, and the responsibilities of leadership have to be taken seriously. This is not always done, and the accidents that result have contributed to making the pursuit of mountaineering seem dangerous to outsiders—which it is not, if proper precautions are taken.

Something of the same sort can be said about accidents in the United Kingdom. A whole crop of deaths on Snowdon at Easter-time recently caused an outcry to be raised in the press. It should be remembered, however, that these accidents occurred to inexperienced walkers who had strayed from the path on a day when there was icing on the slopes. The serious climber attempting difficult walls, who, on account of accidents to walkers, suffers from the opprobrium of the multitude, is not himself liable to such accidents ; rope-work and belaying techniques have now reached such a standard of perfection in England that technical risks are more or less eliminated. In the Alps the risks are of a different kind, and difficulties which can safely be accepted on the smaller English hills have to be avoided and left alone in Switzerland.

Otto Furrer's funeral was due to be held on the day after our return from the Wellenkuppe. Besides being a much-respected guide, he had been world ski champion for several years and possessed a charming personality. His loss was felt by the entire commune, and tributes and cables from all over the world had been pouring in throughout the past twenty-four hours.

As the time for burial drew near, a hush descended on the village. The shops were closed. All social activity ceased. People rose from their chairs or stopped what they were doing at the hotels and lined the streets in silent respect. Except for the roar of the Mattervisp there was a great stillness everywhere.

The cortège came out of the old church which is so much the centre of Zermatt's spiritual life, and in front of it marched the band playing a last tribute to Otto Furrer. Directly behind the band were maidens in white, bearing white flowers. The pall-bearers were six guides, one of whom was Alfons, all dressed in mountain attire, with climbing ropes slung over their shoulders. The four front ones carried ice-axes draped in black, and the two others ski-sticks. The emphasis was obviously on the more serious calling of mountain guide. Behind the coffin moved a procession carrying an absolute torrent of flowers. Every hotel, every guide, almost every family in Zermatt sent its offering.

There were several funeral orations at the cemetery. The President of the Zermatt Guides' Federation made his tribute, followed by a representative of the United Kingdom who spoke on behalf of the Alpine Club, the Alpine Ski Club, and the Ski Club of Great Britain. A representative of the Chamonix guides who had come over specially for the occasion spoke on behalf of his French colleagues, and the last word was had, as it usually is in our earthly lives, by the priest.

I had always looked on the Swiss as a stolid and un-imaginative race, but I was astonished at the depth of sentiment I saw displayed at Otto Furrer's funeral, and at the noble and lyric utterance of those who spoke. Even in the last religious tribute by the priest the phrases showed the inspiration of the summits around, and the poetic similes of mountaineering sounded a note which went straight to the hearts of those who were gathered there in the presence of God and the great peaks. The priest described Otto as " Climbing now to the Everlasting Summit on a divine rope," and ended with the simple but beautiful words, " *Gefallen*

am Berg der Bergen—das Matterhorn !—*wo er zu Hause war* "
(Fallen on the mountain of mountains, the Matterhorn,
where he was as in his own home).

This funeral moved me more than any to which I had
been before. It also showed, with a sudden revelation, how
strong is the faith in Alpine village communities, and how
deep flows the current of feeling—even poetic feeling—
towards the heights above, and the ardour and mystery of
a guide's calling. We are too much inclined to put everything on a basis of commercialism today, but there is no
doubt that the greatest guides are also mountaineers at
heart and hillsmen born.

V

Alfons was saddened by his loss and did not wish to go
out the next day, although we had talked previously of
taking the train to Randa and walking up to the hut for
an assault on the Weisshorn. Gazing sometimes at the
Weisshorn from places like the Taeschalp I had come to
feel that this peak represented a supreme loveliness. The
grace and symmetry of its high-flung summit typified all
that seemed finest in mountain form. Art could not have
contrived anything more fair.

In recent years the Weisshorn has come to be neglected by
ordinary parties. The length of the climb and the primitive
nature of the hut has deterred modern climbers from giving
it the attention which is its due. It has in fact become
" unfashionable," which is perhaps just as well for those
who really go to enjoy the experience of being there.

The weather remained obstinately unpropitious, and day after day we looked at the clouds covering the peaks, and sniffed disapprovingly at the warm Föhn wind, without being able to make a start. Ideas of an eventual ascent of the 'Zmutt Ridge of the Matterhorn began to appear less and less hopeful after constant reports of "Ice on the galleries." I decided we must take a chance in the other direction and go to Randa. After persuading a dubious Alfons, food was bought for a couple of days, and we boarded the 12.05 train from Zermatt.

My rucksack seemed a monstrous weight, what with a large bottle of wine, two books, crampons, and all my "arctic equipment," as well as the food. But after a slow start we began mounting the curves of the Randa path at twelve to thirteen hundred feet an hour. Some way up we rested on an airy ledge directly above Randa village. I gazed through my glasses at the human traces below, already diminished in importance, which would retire progressively from view, and finally vanish altogether as the hours went on. It was another cycle of withdrawal and return which we were now starting, and the thought of the mighty glaciers and ridges above us, over which we would travel on the morrow, added charm to our rest on the ledge.

Higher up we had milk at the last alp before the tree-line, where sturdy Swiss were making cheese in a dark shed. Then we continued onwards by a thin path twisting through abrupt and headlong rocks. We traversed a patch of old snow, then a torrent. More rocks followed. This was no civilised way like the Hörnli or Rothorn tracks, but a lonely mountain trail, giving a singular feeling of isolation. The thunder of a rock-fall on the Dom mingled with the sound of streams from the glaciers. The air grew cold and damp. Clouds hugged the slopes in odd places, and the summit of the Mettelhorn wore a crown of grey.

The rhythm of uphill action carried us slowly higher, until, on a sudden, we saw the side wall of the hut perched on some rocks above us. In half an hour we were there. Six or seven men and one lady climber were in occupation. It was a single room, with straw and blankets to sleep on, one table and a cooking-stove. I felt that this simple hut was more in keeping with our surroundings than the pretentious hostelries of the Rothorn and the Hörnli. It provided shelter and food, a haven from storm and night, which is all that a hut needs to do. The modern thirst for ever-increasing luxury and comfort is somehow not compatible with the true spirit of a mountain voyage, and should be confined to the plains.

There was very little wood fuel at the hut, and its use was strictly reserved for cooking. We made our supper in relays. Alfons cooked soup and spaghetti, which we took with red wine accompanied by sausages and cheese, followed by fruit. A fair meal indeed.

Outside, the weather grew more and more threatening. It was damp and dark, with great clouds chasing across the sky in a continuous stream, cutting off the higher slopes with an indeterminate line. The wind began to howl. Then beating rain and pellets of snow started to lash the hut. Great gusts shook its foundations. We took up our places on the straw, and settled down to what looked like a night of storm. I fell into an uneasy sleep.

An hour or two later the wind had risen to a full gale. The mauve fire of lightning blazed into our small room. The thunder rolled. Sometimes the storm mounted to such

156

The snow-ridge : Zinal Rothorn

a pitch of intensity that we could hardly hear the thunder. The timbers of the hut were heaving and shuddering, and at moments I really thought we were going to be blown off into space, and precipated, hut and all, on to the glacier.

At 1.45 A.M. the harsh clangour of the alarm clock broke across the sounds of storm. No one stirred to stop the ringing. No one moved to get up. A start was out of the question. An uneasy doze followed. The storm went on unabated.

In the grey light of dawn the other occupants bestirred themselves, lit the cooking-stove, and two by two cooked their breakfast and departed, until by seven o'clock the hut was empty.

Alfons was insatiable in his desire and capacity for sleep. A wonderful gift, which is rarely accessible to us more highly evolved and nervous city dwellers. All he could say about eight o'clock was, " I thinks in about half an hour we mounts up and warms our breakfast ; then once more back into the bed we climbs for three or four hours. Otherwise the day he becomes too long."

The weather was grey, with sullen patters of sleet and gusty winds. Low clouds coursed raggedly by, giving a constantly changing pattern of mountain gloom and mountain grandeur, with ridges and peaks being suddenly revealed and as suddenly effaced. The temperature in the hut was down to 42°. Alfons spent most of his time on the straw, while I piled on all my four sweaters and two helmets, Grenfell coat and hood, and sat at the table by the window writing or reading.

After making our lunch of soup and spaghetti, we took advantage of a lull in the sleet to go out on to the glacier, so that I could practise step-cutting on ice and walking in crampons. We did this for about a couple of hours; then the clouds and the snow started coming down, and we returned.

The grey evening wore on, with clouds ever tearing past. Sometimes the valleys below our airy perch were dim and veiled; sometimes their dark depths were revealed, as mists floated stealthily away, only to appear again in a trice, with sudden tendrils and mysteriously swirling shapes.

As the day began to fade I sat at the little window, my elbow propped up on the sill, reading Charles Gos's book of romantic stories, 'La Croix du Cervin.' The poetry and splendour of the mountains, and the lure of the great summits has seldom been more tenderly and beautifully expressed than in the story about Gladys Fairté. The setting was perfect. That small window, looking down on to the fragmentary, elusive and ever-changing, but always sombre mountain scene, added to the art of Charles Gos, gave me an experience of high romance. The inspiration of the hills had never come before in so satisfying a measure. The sense of identification with the spirit of high and lonely places had never been so perfect. There is something in views which are incomplete and changing, hinting at more than they reveal, which the mind never grows tired of; and they are remembered long after the images of completer and more finished effects have crumbled into oblivion.

We cooked an early supper about 6.30 and lay down again on the straw, listening to the wind and the drip and patter of sleet. Prospects for the Weisshorn were all but hopeless. Alfons had already mentally packed his rucksack, ready for Randa and the eight o'clock train to Zermatt on the morrow.

At 10.30 P.M. I woke up and saw stars, though there was still lightning in the east. The sight was encouraging. So I woke Alfons, who sleepily wound back the alarm from 4.45 to 2 A.M., and then immediately turned over and went to sleep.

I got up at two in the morning and went outside. The sky had a misty film over it, high up. A few clouds crouched low over the southern horizon, but the stars showed dimly here and there as diffused patches of light. Underneath the sky the Mischabel peaks showed oddly black. Their jagged summits bit into the heavens with sharply etched lines of snow and rock, rather menacing in their apparent nearness. You could feel they were almost leaning across the valley and watching their solitary human viewer. I felt crushed by the silent presences around and returned to the hut. Alfons said we could start. But I saw that he was anxious. It was obvious even to me that the east ridge of the Weisshorn would be in very bad condition. Another deterioration in the weather would make it more difficult still.

VI

The lantern cast its small, courageous circle of light as I followed Alfons upwards across the frozen snow of the glacier. The slope got steeper and steeper and the rocks ahead grew closer. We came to the bergschrund just as an uncertain dawn began to steal over the sky. Alfons deposited the lantern in an icy recess, and we attacked the rocky couloir ahead of us. The rocks had new snow on them, with a film of ice underneath. Alfon's short crampons bit sharply into the ice and we made rapid progress. The slabs were sloping downwards like the tiles on a roof. Balance was delicate. A long climb up the couloir brought us finally to the glorious east ridge of the Weisshorn.

Looking south, we had an extraordinary view of the Matterhorn and the Dent d'Hérens shining white in new snow against purplish-blue storm-clouds. The lighting gave them a weird effect, for none of the other summits stood out clearly, and the Zermatt Valley was full of dark vapours.

Mists came swirling down to us, followed by a few dry patters of snow. Alfons hesitated, but then decided to continue. " I only take you because you climb well on the descent." We started the ridge. The average gradient of the Weisshorn east ridge is far from steep, but it gave an impression of great sharpness and exposure that day. The rocks were coated with new snow and there was ice underneath. Alfons was in no mood to dawdle. The pace was relentless. We scrambled over towers and sharp points, amid gusts of wind and snow, wearing all our warmest things and two pairs of gloves.

We came to the Grande Gendarme, where Franz Lochmatter fell, and I looked with interest at the gaunt rock which encompassed the end of the greatest guide who ever lived. We turned the gendarme by a complicated crawling manœuvre via a ledge on the north face. The ridge continued beyond. A chain of pinnacles and crags disappeared into clouds ahead, and were lost in the snowflakes that now fell more and more thickly. I began to feel tired at the speed we were climbing and wanted to stop, but Alfons was not in the mood for rests on this day. We went on and on, over the endless

Cutting ste

ridge, until at last I saw the snow ahead where it ended, and the way to the Weisshorn summit lay open.

The snowflakes were falling faster and faster now, and the volleying wind made them patter against our coats. It was intensely cold. The water in the water-bottle slung to my waist under the shelter of my jacket had partly turned to ice, and rattled at each step. Alfons's unshaven beard was clinking with icicles and his eyebrows were rimmed with white.

I had a vision of vast cornices, of a thin swaying crest that soared upwards as we mounted the steep slopes of the snow-ridge. Our pace became slower and slower as my fatigue and the great height began to tell. There were moments of excitement, however, and an exhilaration that overcame every sensation of tiredness when an occasional break in the snow flurries revealed momentarily a far, white summit swimming in a pool of blue sky—remote and alone in the azure. The labour of all the hours, the icy rocks of the ridge and our struggle with cold and snow, seemed as nothing compared with the felicity of attaining that lonely point in space.

The snow-ridge steepened all the time and we hit occasional icy patches where the surface was hard as a dry glacier. The last hour we went slower ; finally we were moving only one at a time on slopes which I realised must be the highest ones.

The sight of the rocks of the Schalli Ridge to our left spelt the end of the climb. I stood with Alfons on the summit of the Weisshorn and felt a glow of deep satisfaction at succeeding in such difficult conditions. We had spent seven hours of continuous effort on the ascent, and, while it was perhaps a disappointment not to be able to stay and enjoy our peak, I felt it was well to see the mountains under all conditions. Experiences of unvarying sunshine, warm rocks, and good views do not give to the mountaineer a rounded or a true picture of the mountain scene. The sterner aspects of storm and cloud are also necessary, not only to bring to the storehouse of experience, but to add to one's insight and discrimination.

After a couple of hurried photos we left the summit and started plunging back along the snow-crest towards the ridge. Alfons kept me on a tight rope and told me to go ahead as fast as I liked. The pleasure of swift and easy movement downhill stood out all the more sharply after the efforts of the last thousand feet of ascent. I think that we must have been back at the start of the ridge within half an hour, as compared with at least two hours coming up this passage.

And the ridge itself seemed easier on the descent, so that it was not so very long before we stood once more at the start of the way down the long couloir. There was more snow on these rocks now, and in the clearer light of day I saw long funnels of polished ice, which obviously acted as a chute for missiles from above. The couloir was a 'fluttersome' experience. I had not been enough in crampons to know that I should strike out boldly and actually walk down the slabs. My instinct was to sit down, but Alfons had complete confidence and told me to go ahead as if I was walking down the road, adding that he could hold me anywhere. So I went down leaning forwards, like a dog tugging at his master's lead, until the bergschrund was reached and Alfons retrieved the lantern. " There, you see, it was easy, after all ! "

The glacier bore us back through scudding flurries of wet snow. The polar air of the highest slopes had been tempered by the proximity of the valley, and Alfons's icicles melted. We entered the hut four hours after leaving the summit, and eleven hours after our departure in the morning. It had been a long day, or perhaps a hard one rather than a long one.

Two hours on the straw revived my organism, and we were down the long descent to Randa in another couple of hours. The evening train bore us slowly into Zermatt, just in time to enjoy one of Mme. Casanova's dinners, with half a bottle of claret, at the Monte Rosa. Herr Alfred Zürcher met me in the street. "What, climbing to-day?" And when I said yes, he congratulated me, adding that the Weisshorn was the only major peak that had "gone" that day.

After dinner I went to the Mont Cervin Bar on one of my rare dancing forays, and met the glamorous Mrs Hafter, a well-known Swiss lady mountaineer. Dark and slim and charming, she leads the life of a widow of means, and reminded me somehow of the heroine in Charles Gos's story. She told me, as we danced, how a few days previously she had ascended the east face of Monte Rosa by the Marinelli Couloir with Alexander Taugwalder. This great expedition was, of course, in a class beyond anything that I could aspire to at this time, but we had an agreeable conversation about the mountains, and I went to bed feeling that the day had embraced a full circle of sensation, from the icy blizzard on the Weisshorn to the gilded mirrors and soft lights of the Mont Cervin.

VII

The Zermatt holiday began to draw to its close. Bad weather succeeded bad weather. The higher summits gathered their defences together and became more and more inaccessible. Day-to-day reports of the state of the 'Zmutt Ridge showed a progressive deterioration; eventually we gave up the idea of attempting it. But I still had my heart fixed on the Mischabel. The idea of climbing the Mischabel Ridge of the Täschorn and making the Dom-Täschorn traverse in a single day occupied my thoughts. To do this and follow it up with the Südlenz-Nadelhorn traverse would certainly round off a good climbing holiday.

Alfons and I left Zermatt on 12th August *en route* for the Täsch Hut. The afternoon was fine and sunny. We were in hopes that the weather had finally relented, and found quite a crowd at the hut, including one woman bound for the Teufelsgrat. Owing to the bad condition of the peaks, Alfons would not agree to try the traverse to the Dom unless another guided rope from Zermatt could be found to accompany us. Eventually the Zermatt guide, Carl Fuchs, and a Swiss alpinist provided the necessary reinforcements; we joined up at supper-time in the evening and then retired early to bed.

Reveille was at 1.45 A.M. The Täsch Hut is comparatively low in altitude and we had an extremely long day ahead. By 2.30 we were out on the glacier, engaged in the classic tramp behind the lantern. The air was still and keenly frosted. Stars blazed. Carl Fuchs was ahead. Alfons and I were the second rope.

The ascent even to the beginning of the ridge is lengthy;

164

dawn was already showing before we had surmounted the Weingarten Glacier and come to the rocks. Between us and the eastern sky towered the steeply toothed, ragged edge of the Mischabel Ridge, cutting us off from the morning glow. And the darkness of the night seemed hardly to have lifted when we noticed the great peaks catch fire, one by one, in the march of day. Monte Rosa, the Matterhorn, the Weisshorn, and then the Breithorn caught the rays—far, blazing points of snow against a mauve morning haze below the blue-green depths of the upper sky.

We climbed the first rocks. Then another stretch of glacier. Finally we stood astride the steep sharp crest which is the Mischabel Ridge of the Täschorn. As we did so mists came trailing up from nowhere, and clouds shut in the sky. We climbed on and on, over rocks covered by powdery snow that turned to ice under the pressure of Vibram soles, always with great care, and dogged by a feeling of insecurity. A wind began to blow.

The whole ridge was festooned with snow cornices—thin and insubstantial attachments that melted silently away at a blow from the axes. The gusts blew a constant stream of frozen crystals into our faces. And the holes in the snow left by the ice-axes of the party ahead were illuminated from below by light shining up through them. It was an odd and rather sinister sight. " *Unheimlich* " was Alfons's comment.

We kept up a steady pace under the encouragement of the guides, and did not stop to enjoy our first halt until over five hours after we had left the hut. In the shade on the west side of the ridge it was altogether too cold to stop ; the wind was blowing with bitter force. The water-bottle on my hip was tinkling with ice. I contrived to thaw it

165

Severe conditions : the Mischabelgrat of the Täschorn
(*See page* 166)

rope and then took a leap. A peal of laughter announced his safe arrival on the snows. Carl drove in his axe and lowered me gently to the lip. It was about ten feet down. The crevasse was very small. I took a jump and landed on all fours, well in safety. The Swiss climber followed, and I managed to snap him in mid-air with my camera. Then Carl, in masterly style, without any reassuring rope from the rear, came walking through the air and landed with barely a jar. The jump brought us on to the Kien Glacier, and from here on we made rapid time.

After traversing the glacier at a good speed, we made the ascent of some wet and slabby rocks whitened by new snow; then plunged down the last snow slopes and ice of the Festi Glacier to the moraines before the Dom Hut.

We entered the Dom Hut about three o'clock, under clearing skies, with the Weisshorn towering up across the valley opposite us. Its serene form set against the afternoon sky seemed a happy omen for our further climb.

VIII

Unfortunately my notes on the Südlenz-Nadelhorn traverse got mislaid, so I have to rely on memory for an account of this day. I remember that reveille at the Dom Hut was once again at 1.45 A.M., and that by 2.30 in the morning we were out on the glacier, tramping the frozen expanses of the Hohberggletscher, *en route* to the Lenzjoch. The comparative lowness of the huts and the scale and size of the peaks in the Mischabel group make the climbs very long ones. Whereas the start of the Hörnli Ridge of the Matter-

" We entered the Dom Hut . . . under clearing skies, with the Weisshorn towering up across the valley. . . ."

horn is just outside the back door of the Belvedere, the Lenzjoch is over four thousand feet above the Dom Hut, and about four hours must be expended in reaching it.

The cold was intense on this morning—the temperature lower, perhaps, than I have ever experienced it anywhere. The air was completely still. The vast concourse of stars glittered above our heads with a frosty, scintillant brilliance. One had a feeling that the solar gift of warmth had vanished for good; that the planet had broken loose from its orbit and was swimming far away in astral solitudes, frigid, unlighted, and dead. In silence we walked through the hushed snowfields, ringed by the watching peaks. And the pale light of dawn saw our two ropes in careful procession under the pendent séracs of the Dom Glacier.

Before us lay the steep, icy slope to the Lenzjoch. Carl Fuchs went ahead making the way. His swift and sure pace, unfaltering, unswerving, showed the expert snow and ice man. He reached the col well before Alfons and I, even though we were merely treading in the steps he had kicked. A glacial wind tore up pieces of the corniced edge and blew them in our faces. Flesh of the face exposed to the air became seared and aching. But the weather was radiantly clear. I had never seen such an amazing display of peaks, such astonishing clarity. In the cold upper air the whole of the Oberland stood revealed; the details were so sharp that one could hardly believe one was looking beyond the Rhone Valley.

We continued climbing up the steep crest on rocks somewhat easier than the Mischabel Ridge of the Täschorn, but equally corniced and rotten in condition. The light from the sun and the brilliance of the air made it a joy to be wrest-

169

ling with such difficulties, and before long we were camped on the summit of the Südlenzhorn, melting frozen limbs away from the wind in a sun of almost dangerous strength. Here we said good-bye to Carl Fuchs and the Swiss climber, whose retreating forms soon disappeared on to the celestial ridge ahead of us.

Alfons and I lazed away a pleasant hour on the summit of the Südlenzhorn, and then looked at the great traverse to the Nadelhorn in front. The ridge was shaded on one side, sunny on the other. Part rocks and part snow, it led down and up in one glorious, exhilarating rush to the peak ahead. To tread it was an adventure, symbolising all the extreme contrasts of existence. On the one hand, light; on the other, darkness. On the one side, cold; on the other, warmth. Careful following of the line of the route spelt Life; but also, on the other side of the appointed way, lay Death. Alfons and I were in no mood to make deviations from the path on this fair day, and we progressed " like gods on the hills together, careless of mankind " along the line of footsteps already traced by Carl.

An hour or so later we stood on the pierced summit of the Nadelhorn, surveying a view of even mightier proportions than the one we had looked at from the Südlenzhorn. We seemed to be floating high in the sky, right among the great peaks, with no trace of the atmospheric effect of recession of planes to show what was nearer and what was farther. We enjoyed a protracted lunch and then scrambled down the continuation of the ridge to the Stecknadelhorn. In spite of a liberal spreading of glacier cream, my face was as red as a tomato and scorched by the ultra-violet rays. Especially painful were the underneath rims of my nostrils,

170

which had caught the light reflected from the snow. Even Alfons found the light more than he could cope with.

The rocks of the Stecknadelhorn leading down to the upper Hohberg Glacier were whispering and clattering with a constant fall of small stones. We made a racing descent, and then sat down on the glacier for a rest, out of range of the small-arms fire of the mountain. The wind had dropped. The sun grilled us in its glare. The Hohberg Glacier was a burning white inferno of light and dangerous ultra-violet rays. Energy sagged as we plodded back in mushy snow.

The early afternoon saw us back at the Dom Hut, and we set off immediately for Randa and the valley. The path is steep: certainly more steep than any other hut-path round Zermatt. In fact Alfons laughingly told me that it is easier to climb the highest mountain in Switzerland (the Dom) than to make the ascent to its hut.

When we came to Randa the houses were lit by a golden evening light, and the church bells were pealing for the Feast of the Assumption. They had been cutting hay in the fields, and the warm, grateful scent reached us before we came into the village. Flowers lay trailing in the grass. An array of geraniums greeted our eyes from the window-boxes. Children were playing happily in the square, and across the valley we saw the Weisshorn Glacier hanging in shade above the pendent torrents that dangled from its lip. It was a scene of human peace and beauty which afforded the perfect complement to the sternness and rigour of the heights. As we sat waiting for the narrow-gauge train to Zermatt I heard a distant sound of singing, and youthful voices rose up in joyful chorus from the church. I felt a great contentment stealing over me.

IX

My climbing holiday was over, but after leaving Zermatt I had a date to meet two old acquaintances and spend my last week-end in Switzerland with them. "The Glacier Express" took me down the curves to Brigue, then up past the Rhone Glacier and the Furka Pass, by what must surely be one of the grandest of all Alpine railway routes. Henri and Gerlinde were waiting for me at Andermatt.

From Andermatt Henri drove us over the Oberalp Pass, down through Sedrun and Disentis ; then into the craggy, tunnelled fastnesses of the Medels Gorge, and up again to the Leukmanier Pass. It was lovely country, and after my twelve-hour drive from Menaggio to Zürich with Henri on an earlier occasion, I felt I had seen quite a lot of Switzerland through the windows of his car.

After the Leukmanier we came down into one of the loneliest stretches of the Tessin, a cold, wind-swept upland of green turf and pines, bordered by the mountains and without a sign of human life anywhere. Henri drew up at the small roadhouse of Acquacalda, where we got out and asked for beds. It was a pleasant, rather new sort of a place, with panelled bedrooms and a great log-fire blazing in the sitting-room. The inn-keeper took us upstairs to some clean and resin-scented rooms, in which we deposited our things ; then we hurried down to the fire.

Henri suggested a walk before supper, but when we got out of the front door the glacial air cut through us like a knife. A heavy wind was blowing scud and wrack through forbidding, snow-pocked mountains, and the arolla pines were creaking in the gale. It must have been near freezing-

" The ridge was shaded on one side, sunny on the other . . ."
(See page 170—Südlenz-Nadelgrat traverse)

point. After about ten minutes' struggle into the teeth of it we turned back. It was a relief to cower round the log blaze after that.

Supper was served early. We had a jolly meal washed down by a bottle of Dôle, reminiscing about old times in Istanbul. Gerlinde was an early childhood companion in Moda, and before she went to Switzerland to get married we had enjoyed a friendship lasting several years. Now she was the mother of a beautiful child and wife to a charming husband. We teased each other and did our best to make the imperturbable Henri jealous, but all to no avail.

The pleasantly varied impressions of the day wandered round my mind as I went upstairs to bed. From outside came the sound of the wind in the pines, and the voice of a stream in the valley. A moon peered fitfully through ragged clouds.

The next day we did more driving. Henri took us down thousands of feet, through many delightful Ticino villages, to the old town of Biasca. From here we turned north again into the valley leading to Airolo and the St Gotthard. This road is a masterpiece of engineering acrobatics, and as we swung into the six-thousand-foot ascent I realised it was the fifth Alpine pass I had done by car with Henri that summer. At Biasca, near the Italian border, it was warm and summery, but on the St Gotthard a bitter wind was howling past from the north. The time was already about 11.30, but Henri was bent on getting Gerlinde onto a rope and taking her up somewhere. We decided on the Fibbia (some nine-thousand-odd feet), which involved an actual ascent of over two thousand. Henri is an experienced climber and I was in perfect training, so poor Gerlinde got the worst of it.

However, we cajoled her up the final easy rocks, and then sat down to enjoy lunch and the view out of the penetrating wind. The snow lay thickly below us. The wind had made its surface icy. We enjoyed some pleasant glissading on the descent, and met up with the car again on the St Gotthard Pass summit at three o'clock.

Henri drove us through Schöllenen and the mighty gorge of the Reuss. Schöllenen is almost grander than the Via Mala, which is generally accorded first place as the most sensational of Alpine chasms.

At the northern end of the St Gotthard tunnel lies the gloomy railway village of Göschenen, walled in by dark cliffs of granite. It was here that I took leave of Henri and Gerlinde and bade them a regretful farewell. They departed to Zürich and I awaited my southern express. About six o'clock I was in the train, travelling through the St Gotthard tunnel, southwards again, and downwards, to Italy.

The afternoon mellowed into a golden evening, and the last light on the mountains by Lake Lugano brought a troubling and exotic loveliness to the close of day on the shores of that tranquil lake. It had been my plan to spend the night at Menaggio, but the last bus to Menaggio had already left by the time the train came into Lugano, so I remained in the carriage and decided to spend the night at Como instead. The express rushed off, onwards down to Chiasso, at the very southernmost tip of Switzerland and just on the border of Italy.

We stopped at Chiasso for the customs. I got out to stretch my legs. And suddenly a different world, a world I had grown away from and almost forgotten, snapped sharply into focus and closed round me. As I stepped into it I felt an altered person. The exhilarated Zermatt feeling evaporated like a puff of smoke in the breeze ; the cold, clean air of the heights, the Monte Rosa Hotel, the tramp of climbing-boots down the street, and the sense of energy and fulfilment—all these things were swept away into the recesses of memory, and, from being part of a present consciousness, were relegated to the past, so that they could now only be seen in retrospect.

The atmosphere of Chiasso gave me one of the most vivid impressions I have ever had. The air was infinitely warm and soft. It had a smoothness that caressed and yet troubled one. I had not experienced warmth at night for so many weeks that it seemed unnatural. A faint breeze whispered through leafy gardens and tall trees—trees growing with all that opulence of foliage and lushness of greenery that one associates with southern climes. Along dusty lanes heavy bushes clambered up the walls, and chickens scrabbled in the dirt. Strange smells were wafted to my nostrils. Dirt was something I had not seen for weeks. There were smart women wandering by in high heels and make-up, coquettish, and walking as if they hardly knew where they were going, or hardly cared. Night crickets trilled a soft harmony, and then again I heard the rustling of the leaves, so different to the sound of pines and mountain firs—more leisurely, gentle, and tentative. The tempo of existence had altered. Here was quietness and indolence. An unwinding of tension. The slow, narcotic spirit of the Lotos-eaters. Of leisure taken languidly and carelessly. Not the active, exhilarated, almost austere leisure of Zermatt.

To return to ordinary life, to southern climates and heat, was like entering a strange, romantic hothouse, sensuous and sweet, but not quite real.

175

I returned to the train and tried to climb back towards Zermatt. But Zermatt had vanished. The crickets trilled and the leaves rustled. A night breeze, smooth like velvet, stirred the curtains of the carriage, and the hum of sounds that came from the plain were lowland sounds, southern familiar noises that told of a day of dust and heat just passed. I gave it up and found myself accepting the new type of world.

The train reached Como about nine. I left my things at the station and wandered into the town. There was an air of fiesta on the place, for it was the Italian August Bank Holiday; the main square by the lake was crowded with people, singing, serenading, cheering, linked arm in arm, and laughing under the stars. A languid, dewy breeze blew in from the lake, and I began to feel sticky and uncomfortable in the close air. In spite of all the gaiety and the songs, I still could not shake myself out of the feeling that life had gone into a sort of trance, torpid and lethargic, beautiful but unreal.

There was no room in any of the hotels. Everyone told me to leave Como and take a train to Milan. But I did not feel inclined to listen to them. Eventually a cheerful Anglican cleric took me in hand and suggested I ascended to Brunate, three thousand feet up, where the hotels might be less crowded. He took me to the funicular, and about 10.30 P.M. I found myself at Brunate, high above the lake. To the north lay the glittering waters; and the expanses of the Lombardy Plain to the south, pricked by the lights of scattered towns and villages fading limitlessly to the horizon, looked like an ocean which had caught reflected on its smooth surface the starry constellations of the sky.

None of the Brunate hotels could take me in, and eventually I got into a deck-chair on the hillside and dozed fitfully under the moon, rather weary and confused, with scattered thoughts circling round all the multiplicity of events and impressions that had distinguished this unusual day : down in the early morning from the glacial rigour of Acquacalda to the warmth of Biasca, then up again six thousand feet to the snows of the St Gotthard ; up still farther on a roped climb of the Fibbia to the snows of an upper world. Down by the Reuss Gorge to Göschenen ; through the St Gotthard tunnel, and down thousands of feet again to Biasca, Lugano, Chiasso, and the heat of Lake Como. And now up to Brunate —all in twenty-four hours.

Somewhere about half-past one or two in the morning the manager of the Albergo Milano sent a flunkey out to me with the message that he could give me a mattress near the bar. Did I want it ? I said yes, and got four good hours' sleep before rising early to climb the Brunate Lighthouse.

Lake Como must surely be one of the most beautiful and romantic places in the world. One could see a large portion of the lake from Brunate Lighthouse, as well as miles and miles of the flat, eternal plains of Lombardy. But what gave me a start was the early morning sunlight picking out, above the haze of the flatlands, the chain of snowfields and peaks that lead from Monte Rosa to the Dom. Tennyson's quatrain came immediately to mind. It fitted so exactly :—

" How faintly flushed, how fantom fair,
Was Monte Rosa hanging there
A thousand shadowy-pencilled valleys
And dewy dells in a golden air."

I realised I was looking for the first time at the mighty east face of the mountain, but the distance was too great

M

for anything much to be seen. Perhaps with the binoculars I might have made out the Marinelli Couloir, but probably not. I felt conscious that the scene had retired from the present tense. It was like looking at Monte Rosa in a book. The view was exquisite, but it no longer touched me directly. The intimacy had withdrawn itself, and the golden haze that veiled the lower hills was also the haze of retrospect; to the extension of space had been added a small, but important, extension of time.

CHAPTER IX

A GLIMPSE OF THE DOLOMITES

DURING the summer of 1952 we were unusually busy at the office, with the result that an Alpine holiday became impossible for me. However, in late September I decided to try and snatch a few days at Cortina d'Ampezzo, and left Istanbul by plane for Rome.

The writings of Leslie Stephen and R. L. G. Irving had inspired an ardent curiosity about the mysterious peaks of the Dolomites, and the lateness of the season had in any case put the higher Swiss summits out of reach.

From Rome I journeyed by train to Venice, gateway to Cortina and the Dolomites. The name Venice had possessed from earliest years a magical sound, and it was a case of love at first sight when I came into contact with this unique city. They say that travellers to Italy become either Romans, Florentines, or Venetians. For me it is Venice that has, of all man-made places, the calmest and most tenderly beautiful appearance. An air of faded and gentle romance pervades it. The past has extended into the present, and offers itself, mellowed by the centuries, yet perfect and intact, to the eye of the watcher. I found in Venice a warm and welcoming atmosphere : an impression also of vividness and light. Its wealth of blended architectural achievement must be hard to equal. And where else in the world can proportions of such grace and loveliness be seen, as upon the Square of Saint Marks ?

I spent a couple of happy days wandering about, mostly on foot, sitting in small cafés at the San Marco, and doing nothing but watch and look. I left sight-seeing *à l'Américaine* for another and future visit. From the start I had felt at home. To find one's way from place to place there seemed the easiest thing in the world, whereas Rome has always produced in me an impression of noise and great confusion.

From the top of the Campanile on the second afternoon I caught a distant glimpse of the spiky peaks of the Dolomites. The weather gave a promise of good climbing on the steep walls of magnesian limestone, where my imagination had wandered so often, and on the following morning the bus left the Piazzale Roma in Venice for Cortina d'Ampezzo.

After threading the four-mile bridge across the lagoon to the mainland we started running through the verdurous and smiling Campagna towards the Alpine foothills. Four hours later I was up among the rocky summits of the Cortina ambit.

The Dolomite scenery filled me with astonishment. Never before had mountains like this swum into my ken. That first evening from Faloria I watched the spectacle of a red sun flashing its rays on to the silent congregation of spires and precipices, frozen, one felt, into merely temporary equilibrium, and awaiting only the shades of night to enter into some unearthly activity. Mountains in a trance, unnaturally muted, they stood there in the clear air with a kind of soundless immobility, at variance with all my other experience of great peaks. The purple clouds played on the high red towers, but the voice of the stream was thin and far away. No muffled thunder of the glacier torrent, no distant crash

of falling stones reached the ear to remind one of the destructive play of mighty forces ; these Dolomite walls seemed exempt from the natural fate of hills—from the violence of erosion and decay which forever assail the greater heights of the Alps.

I returned for dinner to the Hotel de la Poste, where I asked the porter to recommend me a guide : I wanted someone mature in years, steeped in the traditions of his own hills and devoted to the craft. The porter bowed slightly, " I will call for Celso Degasper, sir."

Celso arrived in time for a liqueur. He was tall and dark, very slim, with grey hair and a most distinguished mien. I took to him from the start, and soon came to see that he was a superb cragsman, with a style far superior to anything I had met before. Celso had a certain amount of livestock and owned an attractive house on the Via Roma ; in the off-seasons he worked as a joiner, and the polished hardwood furniture in the house was all of his own hand. He guided in the summer because he was a born mountaineer, and had felt the call of the hills from earliest years. Several routes carry his name, bearing witness to daring and enterprise, as well as skill.

The season had ended in Cortina. The Hotel de la Poste was all but empty. I felt somewhat dejected at the prospect of no one to talk to and no apparent chance of meeting a new companion; but Celso's friendly presence and the conversation about routes and climbs brought a pleasant excitement to the first evening.

I went upstairs to bed thankful to have had even the brief opportunity of reaching the mountains again in '52, and wondering how I would make out on the morrow amid

Autumn clouds, near Cortina

the vertical limestone pitches of the Cinque Torri. With Celso that evening I had run into the system of climbs graded in terms of difficulty—grade I. being very easy, and grade V. representing the extreme limit of unaided human possibility. There is also a sixth grade (*sesto grado !*) reserved for climbs so difficult that they can only be surmounted with the aid of mechanical devices. The Torri of the morrow were grade III.

Though I shall never be a good cragsman I found the physical exhilaration of pure rock-climbing to be even more intense than that of greater mountaineering. The rough, easy rock, and the astonishing steepness and exposure of the routes, proved a heady, almost intoxicating potion. I followed Celso, watching his light aerial flitting from hold to hold, lost in wonder at the smooth flow of his upward rhythms—effortless, unhalting, and graceful. It represented the pure joy of movement, linked to something of the excitement of dancing, as I tried to move smoothly rather than fast, effortlessly rather than with power. We glided up the steep needle of the Torre Inglese and took off from its summit on a doubled rope. When Celso airily dismissed this as a beginner's scramble I realised that Dolomite standards were altogether different from Swiss standards. The climbing here was steeper, harder, and more exposed. Standards of cragsmanship were more developed. Yet the risks were undoubtedly less. Wind, weather, and the time factor ; snow and ice and falling stones hardly came into the picture. I suppose that if I were to visit Wales or the Lake District I should find climbing being done of even higher standard than the Dolomite routes. It is a truism of mountaineering that the lowest climbs are apt to be the most difficult technically, and at the same time the safest; by the time one reaches the Himalaya, climbing is on the whole very easy technically, but at the same time exposed to considerable danger.

I had become used among the great peaks to the two-day climb, to the rhythm of withdrawal and return, to the sense of pilgrimage and achievement. Here in Cortina it was different. Instead of the pre-dawn start from the hut, one rose from the luxury of a hotel bed to enjoy a leisurely breakfast; and this was the prelude to a short day's climbing which ended in the comforts of a hot bath the same evening. The imperious urgency of time, the demands on pace and endurance, the glory of stars and sunrise, and the lofty visions of the upper world which the Alpine day demands and confers, were missing here. The many imponderables of route conditions, speed and weather, which give to greater mountaineering its satisfying uncertainty and variety, were ruled out. What was in other places the vocation, appeared here more in the light of a sport.

Cortina itself, lying on the main Dolomite Road and swept by the clangour of vehicles, lacked altogether the calmness of Zermatt. For despite all modernised amenities it is still possible, without being too fanciful, to endow Zermatt with a certain spirituality. Its village life centres on the church and is bounded by the great peaks. Incense is burnt on the high altars of mountain endeavour, and one feels round one the atmosphere of a long and proud tradition dedicated to the service of the hills.

There must be many valleys in the Dolomites, like the fastnesses of Primiero, where the mountain voices still speak in the old unsullied accents of primeval beauty. To enjoy these places, however, one needs the right companion, or a readiness to wander alone. And lack of the former has contributed to deflecting me towards the more popular centres in the hope of finding there the companionship no longer available, except on very rare occasions, in a workaday life which is thousands of miles from the amenities of climbing-clubs and a respect for nature.

With these thoughts in mind I trudged down the Falza-reggo Pass road with Celso after an exhilarating morning on the Torre Inglese and the Torre Grande. Celso seemed to believe I climbed quite well and was enlarging on the delights of a "real ascension," which he was looking forward to showing me. This was the south wall of the Punta Fiamès, route Dimai-Verzi.

I looked across the valley and saw a sheer face bounding up a couple of thousand feet from the plinth of screes to the jagged crest. The view of the Punta Fiamès inspired respect. I enjoyed the sound of its name, but was dubious at the sight of that ruthless precipice. My Alpine climbs had all been ridge ascents, which conditions only had rendered difficult. This was another matter. And a fourth grade climb of a Dolomite wall seemed rather a presumptuous undertaking. However, Celso thought otherwise, and his friendly charm and confidence won me over. We decided on the Punta Fiamès for the morrow, without taking into account that the sunshine we had enjoyed on the Cinque Torri was to be the last fine weather of the season.

On the morrow it poured sullenly all day. Swollen clouds, which had sucked up their burden of moisture above the far Adriatic, pressed heavy on Cortina, and the mountains were swallowed up.

We set out the morning after in cold, damp atmosphere,

towards the wall of the Punta Fiamès. A gap in memory has blurred much of the ascent even at this short distance in time. But I remember the grey slabs and cracks, the narrow ledges ; the subtle evasiveness of the route, and the impression of overwhelming steepness ; Celso's rope disappearing into impossible heights above me, until it seemed thin as a string in the distance ; the struggles over a craning immensity of space, and the occasional frightening traverses athwart the leaning wall, where my heavy boots seemed incapable of adhering, and where Celso cat-footed across in *kletterschuhe* as if he was on the hotel parapet.

Before we got to the notorious and evilly reputed Black Chimney, a white film came stealing across the valley and the roofs of Cortina faded from view. I looked again and saw a swirl of snowflakes sailing upwards in our direction. Soon the dry rustle of tiny pellets was all round us and my fingers became chilled and aching. Celso gave careful directions about how to tackle the overhanging chimney ; I watched him swing up between the dark walls with almost unbelievable agility.

The Black Chimney delayed us nearly half an hour, for my efforts must have been anything but pretty to watch. Celso was entirely unperturbed by the snowstorm and determined to avoid indulging in the good old sport of " hauling up one's tourist." I did not approve of this so much at the time, poised between earth and sky above fifteen hundred feet of the Punta Fiamès face, but have since appreciated his feeling, which was a wish to instruct rather than merely guide. Eventually I emerged worn and breathless on to a narrow stance above the chimney, to meet a smiling Celso, grey hair whitened by the snow, and wearing an expression of confidence and slightly amused pleasure on his handsome face. " Not fair, Celso, far too difficult," I said.

" Ah yes, but, you see, you did it. That is grade four. The Black Chimney. Other climbs come easy to you now."

Our position did not exactly appear to me to inspire confidence. It was snowing harder than ever ; visibility had shrunk to fifty yards and the clouds had closed in around us. Below the Black Chimney the drop could only be measured in terms of the three strenuous hours we had spent on the wall. Above us, dimly seen through snow and cloud, a vast overhang boomed out.

" We pass by the side of him," murmured Celso, puckering his brow. " The weather becomes a little bad. We must continue."

Another half-hour of steep but faster climbing brought us to the summit ridge of the Punta Fiamès, north of the summit. The snow was falling thicker still and the rocks were white. We scrambled quickly to the top. Celso extended a thin but powerful hand. " So ; not for many years do I climb the Punta Fiamès in such weather."

I looked for my watch to see the hour, and noticed to my surprise that I was no longer wearing it. A Zenith watch was a valuable possession and its loss was unfortunate, to say the least. We agreed that it must have been wrenched off my wrist in some difficult passage ; then we left the summit to descend the easier rocks down to the scree gully.

The light screes bore us down to the valley in a swift if hardly soundless rush. I found to my pleasure that I was almost Celso's equal in scree-running, and we raced down a thousand feet in five minutes of muscle-wearing but wholly joyful action. Down among the dripping larch-woods the path to Cortina led us home through torrents of rain. Wet through and cold outside, I felt within an ecstatic glow.

II

The weather was so bad the two following days that I decided to break my stay in Cortina and travel to Zürich and Berne, where I had some business to transact for our firm.

When I returned to Cortina for a last three days of holiday I went into a stationery shop the first afternoon and was immediately addressed by the assistant. " Surely you are the English gentleman who was climbing with Celso ? " " Right," I answered. " What about it ? " I could hardly believe my ears when the assistant replied, " Oh, there is good news for you about your watch. Celso climbed the Punta Fiamès alone on Sunday and found it caught in a crack."

The precious Zenith was brought in by Celso in person after dinner, still ticking and in perfect order. He had found it in the neighbourhood of the Black Chimney ; the strap had parted and the watch was securely wedged in the rocks. A rather remarkable episode.

The following day I bought some *kletterschuhe* and wandered up the Falzareggo Pass road with Celso, *en route* for the Torre di Falzareggo. This handsome obelisk affords a good climb and Celso had promised me a " descent *en rappel* most interesting " from the summit. The *kletterschuhe* fitted perfectly ; a few fitful gleams of sun encouraged us to think of better weather ahead. I found the Torre di Falzareggo splendid climbing, and doing it in thin shoes after the Punta Fiamès made me feel a sense of mastery which I could not have achieved previously. Before we had reached the summit it had started to snow again, but we were both in high spirits and swung up the last pitches with a gay abandon.

The snowflakes crowded in round us while we stood on the final peak. Celso prepared things for the *rappel*. We climbed down a little, as far as a piton; the rope was threaded through; then I found myself poised outwards over the brink, about to do the longest double rope descent I had ever tried. " Loosely with the right hand," said Celso, as I gripped the rope in front of me. " Off you go. . . . Looser with the right hand. . . . Faster, faster, faster ! " By the end, as the friction got less, I was moving quite respectably, but still not fast enough to please Celso.

I unroped on the platform below, then watched him pitter-patter down that smooth wall of vertical rock in one unbroken flow of easy movement, effortless as a bird and almost as swift. It was a wonderful sight. We pulled the rope through the piton and continued down a rock gully to the slopes leading towards the road. Cortina lay seven or eight miles away, and the snow had turned to sleet. We walked squelching back to the hotel, where I disappeared upstairs immediately to enjoy a leisurely bath.

Our final expedition in Cortina was to be the Monte Cristallo, whose height now put it almost certainly out of bounds. Celso believed the last five hundred metres would be iced, but we decided to try nevertheless.

A car was arranged for 4.30 A.M. to take us to the Tre Croce Pass, and the pre-dawn start made it feel like real mountaineering. The day was frosty and crisp. From the

188

" *Above us, dimly seen through cloud and snow, a vast overhang boomed out . . .*"

(*See page* 186—*Punta Fiamès, south wall*)

Tre Croce we had a fair vision of the three Tofanas transfixed in the pink glare of morning. The Piz Popena Ridge caught the rays as we mounted the path towards the gully between the Piz Popena and the Cristallo. On our left a group of startled chamois fled for the rocks.

We were moving on very steep, pebbly slopes when the sun peeped over the ridge ; within seconds the whole gully began to rustle and rattle. Streams of pebbles, unleashed from the imprisoning ice, entered into activity about us until the earth itself seemed to be in movement. We heard a high-pitched whine from the Cristallo wall on our left, followed by an echoing crash ; this was succeeded by several whines of different pitch—then, several smaller cracks like a whip-lash. The mountain artillery, normally silent in these hills, seemed to be operating in force that morning. We moved hurriedly over into the protecting shade of the Piz Popena. The snow here was deep ; the higher we mounted towards the col the thicker it became and the steeper the slope. An intense cold chilled the limbs. The air was still, but as we climbed a dull booming sound came to our ears from the col. We looked up and saw a sparkling plume of snow crystals flying high in the sun-swept air above us ; already their icy dust was falling on our jackets. Everything showed that the wind was at work in majestic force.

Putting on all our spare pullovers and an extra head covering, we roped up.

A traverse followed to the Cristallo side of the couloir. Celso cut steps. Occasional arctic gusts of wind smote us with savage force. The rocks presented an astonishing sight, being literally encased in ice. Our progress became very slow.

Gradually we worked our way on to the wide terrace that skirts the base of the summit pyramid of Monte Cristallo. Underneath was ice. All round us the rocks flashed in glassy sheets, and across the Tre Croce Pass to our south the Sorapis-Punta Nera group shone with a white and frosty glitter. Then, for the third time on this holiday, it began to snow, and wind-driven tatters of cloud started tearing through the col on a level to the east of us. We had traversed about three-quarters of the terrace at this stage when Celso spoke the word for retreat. The Cristallo summit still lay about a thousand feet above, guarded by impassable pitches of glazed rocks.

Celso smiled, " Even in winter I do not see so much snow and ice. But it has been good. A real mountain day."

As we wended our way not too regretfully back to the couloir and made a kick-heel descent of the snow-slope, I felt that it had indeed been a good day. The fullness of the mountains had welcomed and braced us: the climbing up to the realms of light in the early hours; the joy of perfect muscular co-ordination; the sense of health and fitness; the companionship; the calmness of soul; wind and rock and snow, and the glory of lofty peaks—it had all been there.

For a moment there had been a fear in my mind that I was falling victim to the facile thrills of the cragsman who becomes a rock technician to the exclusion of all else. But the modest pleasures of the Cristallo showed again the truer and more lasting values. The whole is greater than the part, and undue emphasis should be avoided.

CHAPTER X

THE MARGHERITA HUT AND THE
ROAD BEYOND

JULY of 1953 saw me once again in Cortina d'Ampezzo, *en route* to the peaks of Switzerland. As the bus turned up into the Ampezzo Valley I was greeted with cold winds and sleet, and the news which came through that evening about conditions in the western Alps was far from encouraging. It is one of the advantages of the Dolomites, though, that climbing is possible there, no matter what the weather.

For a long time I had been fascinated by the lordly title of Tre Cime di Lavaredo—perhaps the only Italianisation which is an improvement on the old Austrian name—and the vision in photos of those three amazing northern precipices had consumed the winter months of mountain quietude in Istanbul. The Tre Cime are one of the most remarkable groups in the Dolomites, and when I told Celso of my wish to see them he was quick to share my enthusiasm. The Innerkofler-Elversen traverse of the Cima Piccola di Lavaredo was suggested as the minimum we should aim at.

While training on the abrupt slabs of Torre Lusi we met the Austrian film director, Louis Trenker, with a whole cohort of actors, actresses, and guides. They had been trying to make a mountain film on the Cinque Torri, but out of fourteen days at the Rifugio di Cinque Torri, only two had been suitable for filming. Trenker was just about to return to Cortina in disgust. One of the attached guides told me with a resigned look that the actresses had been displaying "*viel temperament*," and Celso and I both smiled at the thought of expensive artistes enduring for so long the frigid discomfort of a mountain refuge.

Two days later we drove to the Misurina Lake *en route* for Cima Piccola. The Tre Cime summits were blotted in cloud, but here and there blackened ribs were showing through the mists, which gave an impression of cold malevolence.

We attacked the rock at eleven o'clock, and after an initial strenuous overhang, seemed to float easily up through wisps of cloud as far as the little col by the Punta Frida. The last five hundred feet of the north wall of Cima Piccola bounded up from here in airy verticality. We could momentarily see the whole face, and I was taken aback at its steepness. Celso rested for five minutes, then took off. We swarmed up a succession of chimneys and cracks. Intricate little traverses and changes in direction made me realise that these routes are for leading by experts only. The exposure was extraordinary. One's toe was to the rock, but the heel often dangled in the void, over mists through which could be seen, at an immense distance below, the snowfield at the base of the precipice.

It was strenuous climbing, but exhilarating, and nowhere were the traverses extended enough to make me feel nervous. As we got higher the dark fang of the Punta Frida began to sink beneath us into its base of swirling vapours; and the sinister "outside edge" of Cima Grande di Lavaredo glinted oddly through the mists, suggesting umplumbable depths below and unscalable heights above. It was a strange experience being surrounded by the half-revealed and half-concealed presence of all these spires and precipices.

Quite suddenly we came to a level platform ; and there we were on the summit of Cima Piccola di Lavaredo. It was the smallest and narrowest peak I have ever seen.

One guided party had preceded us. The other guide, with an Italian climber, had brought an eighty-metre *corde de rappel*. He kindly offered to let us use it so that we could do the long *rappel* from the summit in one fell swoop. This was the longest double-rope descent I have ever made. It was more than one hundred and fifteen feet and partly in free air. To gaze up from the security of the stance on the south face where the *rappel* ended and watch Celso taking flight downwards was a privileged moment.

We rattled down the rest of the descent, and were home in Cortina for tea. Celso was emphatic that the south wall of Tofana di Rozès lay within my powers ; and as the sight of this face from Cinque Torri had attracted me the previous year, we decided on it for the day after the morrow.

The Tofana south face is a bigger proposition than Cima Piccola, and constitutes one of the classic Dolomite "*grandes courses.*" Celso was careful to avoid mentioning the famous traverse except in vague terms, and as I had not read Smythe's last book I was unprepared for what to expect.

We left Cortina at five in the morning, accompanied by a junior guide who was to carry the rucksacks and mountain boots to the summit by the ordinary route. A couple of hours later we had surmounted the screes, put on the rope, and donned our rubbers. Clouds covered the upper part of the face, but the weather did not look too unhopeful.

We started the climb by crawling along an overhung

N

gallery, and then through a gaping hole that brought us on to a thousand-foot face of easy slabs. These led up to the First Amphitheatre, which was a spot I was longing to view from close at hand. A study of Tofana from Cinque Torri had shown it to be an impressive eyrie gouged out of the face, and surrounded by absolutely vertical precipices a couple of thousand feet high.

Unfortunately, when we got there, mists obscured the upper continuation of the rock, and all we could see were ribbed and banded walls of awesome steepness disappearing into the clouds. The snow on the floor of the amphitheatre was frozen hard. Like scalded cats we dashed across the fifteen or twenty feet of its surface to the security of the rocks on our left. Celso had no need to tell me of the danger. I could see that if the sun warmed the summit of Tofana the place would become exposed to stone-falls. It is for this reason that the guides usually aim to cross the amphitheatre before 9 A.M. We crossed it at 8.30, then continued climbing on more difficult rocks for half an hour till we had passed the so-called Second Amphitheatre, and sat down to rest underneath an overhanging yellow wall. Just before we did so there was a roar like thunder from the clouds above. The rock walls boomed and reverberated to the crash of boulders, and part of the mountain that had broken off went splintering down the shute of the First Amphitheatre. Celso said nothing, but the muscles on his face tightened.

Above us on the yellow wall was a passage of exceptional severity. Celso surmounted it by a little force and a great deal of skill, but when it came to my turn it was only by the most extreme exertion and help from the rope that I got up. "Something very similar fifth grade," said Celso with a smile as I panted for breath on the next stance.

We continued climbing for another three-quarters of an hour before coming to a level platform of screes. I could not see what happened beyond; all above and around, the pitches were vertical or impossibly overhanging. The place looked like a trap. It was only here that Celso broke the news. " Here you have a good rest, and then we make the traverse—about forty metres." I could hardly believe my ears. Forty metres. Where could there be security on such a passage ?

It started gently enough, on broad ledges about a foot wide, which narrowed until we came to a crucial place in the centre of the traverse where a piton afforded reassurance. The exposure was enormous and terrifying. I cannot remember ever experiencing such an immediate threat to my instinct for self-preservation, or feeling so frightened. To follow a resolute leader up a wall, however steep, is not any strain on the nerves : falling off means a drop of a few inches. But coming off on a traverse means the shock of a long fall on the rope, then the swinging like a pendulum and the battering to and fro on the slabs—IF one is held.

I now know that this traverse on the Tofana is notorious for affording one of the two or three most exposed situations in Alpine climbing.

Celso left me threaded to the piton and went his leisurely, horizontal way along another sixty feet, poised in delicate adhesion with the rock-face, above the enormous drop below. Not a sign of worry or undue concentration disturbed his features. He disappeared round a corner, then announced that the traverse had ended and that he was going up sixty feet to a firm stance and piton : I was not to move or untether myself.

The minutes went by and a cold wind added to my shivering. Eventually the rope began to flick over the rocks until it formed a straight line to my left, about forty degrees from the vertical, before disappearing over the overhang. A thin voice floated down. I thought it said " Ready ! " but could not be sure. It was some time before we could make each other understood. After I was quite certain that all was well I snapped open the karabiner and freed my rope from the security of the piton. It was up to me now to go it alone ; without advice or directions ; without Celso's presence to encourage. Alone on the wall. For a long time I could not part from the friendly piton or commit my limbs to action. My legs and arms seemed paralysed.

A faint call came down the line, " Make your start, I am in strong position." I forced myself away from the piton and began, clinging fiercely to the rock in defiance of all Celso's teachings. As I progressed the rope flicked leftwards across with me. I tried to forget what was below and concentrate on the increasing verticality of the rope's lie. When its deviation from the vertical became reduced to twenty degrees I breathed again. The last few yards were easy ; the rope led straight up to Celso, still invisible above. Finally the intervening steep pitch was surmounted and I saw him well and truly anchored at his stance.

The rest of the climb was pure delight. A succession of chimneys and ribs led us surely upwards and the difficulties were nowhere beyond my standard. A last overhanging chimney brought us up on shaly slabs leading to the final ridge before the peak. At five minutes past twelve we stood in deep snow beside the cross that marks the summit of Tofana di Rozès.

Our rucksacks, warm clothing, and mountain boots

awaited us. Also an ample lunch, to which we all did justice. I told Celso I believed he had made a mistake in taking me on the traverse while I was still a relatively inexpert climber : it was something which only a couple more seasons of experience could have fitted me for. But Celso merely grinned and said the traverse was a valuable experience which would harden me against ever being frightened again.

However, I had my revenge by descending the two thousand one hundred feet of rock to the Cantori Refuge in thirty-five minutes, and leading the guides down the further three-thousand-five-hundred-foot descent from there to Pocol in another thirty-five.

After dinner we gathered convivially at the Hotel de La Poste for liqueurs and coffee, to talk of Dolomite climbing history and Celso's sixth-grade climbs. Plans for a following summer were touched on, and I left Cortina the next morning with a pleasantly satisfied feeling.

II

It was my intention after Cortina to seek a complete change from rock, and turn to the snow and ice routes of the Oberland ; but a friendly letter from Betty Glenn in Zermatt, and news that some old acquaintances were at the Monte Rosa Hotel, made me change plans. I sent an SOS to Fraulein Eberhardt to put me up in the annexe.

The great peaks greeted me back with special intimacy. It was like a happy home-coming to reach Zermatt again and sit down to a meal under Mme. Casanova's watchful eye in a largely English dining-room. Alfons came to visit me in the evening and listened with interest to the list of

On the forty-metre traverse : Tofana di Rozès, south wall

my Dolomite climbs. We discussed the possibilities of the 'Zmutt Ridge, and I was astonished to learn that the Matter-horn had not been climbed yet : the summer had been unusually wet and cold, and the accumulation of snow on the " roof " was unprecedented in living memory.

I decided to give up the idea of the 'Zmutt Ridge. To satisfy an old ambition and spend a night at the Margherita Hut after climbing Monte Rosa seemed an even more attractive and certainly more feasible alternative. The Margherita is the highest and remotest hut in the Alps. Its altitude above sea level is actually greater than the summit of the Matterhorn, and only a few feet below the fifteen thousand mark. Around it for miles, north and south and west, extend the vast snow and ice fields of the Monte Rosa complex.

I suggested to Alfons that we should do a big expedition of forty-eight hours, taking in Monte Rosa (Dufour), the Zumsteinspitze, the Signalkuppe, the Lyskamm, Castor, Pollux and the Breithorn, all of which are snow and ice peaks. We agreed to wait for better conditions, and Alfons advised me in the meantime to practise crampon work on the glaciers.

The Monte Rosa Hotel provided good company and a few pleasant days of minor climbs and glacier excursions followed.

On 26th July I bought food for three days and took the train to Rotenboden after lunch. Alfons followed later. In a leisurely manner I made my way across the Grenz Glacier to the Bétemps Hut, just as a shower of hail began to patter on to the ice.

The Bétemps is low. Looking out towards the Matter-horn one feels crushed there by the tremendous ice-slopes to the left; for thousands of feet the hanging glaciers and milk-snow precipices tower above one in the extended line of north faces thrown down by the Lyskamm, Castor, and Pollux. They are frosted with a permanent shroud of virgin white. The sun has no influence in these sanctuaries of tragic cold, whose silence and immobility are disturbed only by the occasional rumble of an ice avalanche.

The hut was full. There must have been eighty or ninety people there, the majority of them bound for Monte Rosa. We had an early supper and retired to bed, with the alarm set for 1.45 A.M. Outside, a full moon silvered the mountains.

Next morning we were outside by a quarter to three, negotiating the boulders and screes up to the glacier. Unroped and without a lantern, I followed Alfons in the track of numberless other parties, across rocks and hard-frozen snow, in the bright light of the moon. A bitter wind blew from the south.

An hour later we roped up on the glacier as the first flush of dawn began to steal over the peaks. Above the Breithorn the moon hung silvery-cold, while Castor and the Matterhorn lighted up with an orange glow in the march of day. The wind was so violent that snow particles were being lashed into our faces by the gusts. We pressed steadily on, past fantastic strata of ice and snow-muffled crevasses which went down like the vortex of a whirlpool into the hidden depths of the glacier. It was a frozen world, utterly silent save for the wind, and different from any mountain I had been on before in the completeness of its sense of isolation. The parties ahead were lost in a flurry of snow-ridden gusts and their presence was felt rather than seen.

We came to a steep ice-slope, curving round a corner to

the south. Here we took out our crampons and strapped them on. In the terrible wind my hands became numb almost immediately and we lost half an hour before I could complete the job. During this time seven or eight parties came past, returning to the Bétemps after giving up the climb. The cold and the wind had been too much for them. Two men were frostbitten, the result of wearing faulty gloves. Alfons asked me what I wanted to do, and said, "I don't think anyone climb Dufour to-day." I told him that he and I would do it.

We continued upwards on steeper slopes, under tremendous gusts of wind so violent that one had to drive in one's axe, lean forward on the gale, and remain motionless for minutes on end. More parties passed us on their way back until I judged we were the only rope left on the ascent. The sun shone fitfully between tearing clouds through the icy spume of driven snow.

It was already high morning when we reached the beginning of the rock-crest which forms the last hour of climbing on Monte Rosa. The wind was now at its worst and the cold was extreme. I was wearing two woollen helmets under my Grenfell hood, but the force of the snow-laden blasts seared the exposed skin on my face. At one moment we would be climbing in clean motionless air, and the next second a hurricane gust would hit the ridge, tearing up particles of ice in a paroxysm of fury. These squalls came with absolutely no warning and, if we had not exercised care, would have blown us clean off the crest. On level, exposed places I learnt to cultivate a squat, splayed-out walk which foiled the treachery of the wind. The suddenness with which the gusts subsided was almost more dangerous than the speed of their onslaught. One would be leaning out against the blast, and when it stopped the effect made one overbalance, just as a person would who was leaning against a support that was suddenly removed. But it was an exhilarating struggle. The elements were doing their best to keep us off Monte Rosa, and we were winning through to our goal none-theless. The vision of a night in the Margherita spurred me on more than the ambition to ascend the Dufourspitze.

We had been at grips with the rock-ridge for about ten minutes when we met the guide Otto Taugwalder and a Swiss alpinist, M. Génequand of Geneva. We asked them if they had been to the top and they replied that no one had; they had had enough themselves and were coming back. M. Génequand had originally been bound like us for the Margherita and the Lyskamm traverse, and as Alfons was keen to have a second guided rope to help with step-cutting on the Lyskamm, he tried to persuade Otto Taugwalder and M. Génequand to change their minds. Eventually they agreed to turn round and resume the ascent with us. Alfons and I led the way.

Owing to occasional patches of ice and snow we were still wearing crampons, and I found rock-climbing with my long-clawed Eckensteins quite a novel type of activity. The thundering gusts of wind and the condition of the crest made it more delicate than it usually is, but we contrived to make respectable progress. As we got farther up the wind became less dangerous and the going pleasanter.

At half-past nine we stood on the highest tip of the Dufourspitze. Monte Rosa was at our feet. I had climbed beyond the fifteen-thousand-foot mark for the first time in my life, and ascended the second highest peak in the Alps.

In all directions beneath us extended the enormous upper glaciers and snowfields, an expanse as desolate as the arctic, and seemingly as far removed from the haunts of men.

We sat on the top for half an hour, then began the descent of the ridge down to the Zumsteinspitze Col. This was more difficult than the ascent, but though Alfons and I took more than an hour and three-quarters to negotiate it, Taugwalder and M. Génequand, who had started with us, were only half-way down when we reached the col. Turning back, we looked onto the profile of the fearsome Marinelli Couloir on Monte Rosa's east face. Alfons paused and pointed out to me the spot where Otto's brother, Alexander Taugwalder, had fallen while descending it the previous summer. The Marinelli Couloir was his special climb. He was the leading exponent and acknowledged premier expert on the route. I should hardly call the couloir a "standard climb." Its ascent demands great endurance, icemanship and skill, as well as luck. When Alexander decided to descend it, heads were shaken at the Bétemps, and it was felt he might be straining his good fortune. He left the hut with his alpinist at 10 P.M., and it was the last time they were seen alive.

Mrs Hafter, whom I met after climbing the Weisshorn, had travelled to Zermatt for his funeral, and drove her ice-axe into the ground by his grave, with the single word, "Fertig," meaning that she would never climb again. Alexander Taugwalder had been her personal guide on numberless ascents, and the gesture was profoundly respected by the guides in Zermatt.

We ascended from the col to the summit of the Zumstein-spitze, and then saw clearly ahead of us, on its airy pedestal of rock, the wooden railing and the windows of the Margherita Hut—my goal for the day.

The snow had got mushy by this time and the sun had already southed. The unbroken hours of effort in the thin air at this great height had begun to tell on me. Even Alfons seemed a bit the worse for wear after his battering in the wind on the Dufourspitze Ridge. The sun was shining through light mist and the snows reflected it with redoubled force until the upper glacier we walked on became a white inferno of blinding glare. As we stood on the shallow col between the Zumsteinspitze and the Signalkuppe, preparing to ascend our third summit of Monte Rosa that day, I realised that the last three hundred feet would be an extreme effort. We ascended by slow degrees in steps already cut, pausing every five paces for breath. The wooden rail came nearer and nearer. Finally it was grasped. We stood on the platform of the Margherita, on the summit of the Signal-kuppe. I stopped for a moment to marvel at its position and the temerity of the men who had built it ; then entered the narrow door.

Eleven hours had passed since we had eaten breakfast, but I decided against a meal at this moment and clambered up the rung steps to a cramped sleeping-room above. It was a haven after the storm. Rest after action. A bunk to lie on. The air was motionless and cold. The burning glare of the snowfields had been excluded. Through a single small window one could see a vignette of glacier-névé and rocks ; then extremely far below, and misted into the distance of thicker atmosphere, the valleys of Italy. No sign or trace of human beings.

We made our greeting to the young Italian hut-keeper and lay down. A couple of hours later Taugwalder and M. Génequand arrived to join us. My pulse was hammering away at a steady 110, and I did not stir until the sun had wested and I heard the hut-keeper shovelling snow for the evening pot of tea.

For tea-supper I kept to milk, cornflakes and tinned fruit-salad, as well as some yoghurt from Zermatt. Alfons was scandalised at my refusing tea and soup, but then my food habits have always been a source of despair to guides; and tea did not seem very appetising, made from melted snow, with the miserably low boiling-temperature of water at fifteen thousand feet above sea level. The room was dark but the stove sizzled cheerfully, and after the long rest my appetite was keen. Besides the hut-keeper there was an Italian resident meteorologist, and we all sat down together and talked with an animation and intimacy which took wings from the remoteness of our position. As the occasional gusts whistled through the outer boards, one had the feeling of complete apartness from terrestrial contact.

I got up to see the final crimson of evening on the snows. The day began to fade over the immense frozen waste below us, and in the sky the constellations lit up. The thermometer sank lower and lower. I had never before felt so far removed from earthly bonds, so near to the sidereal universe. The astral solitudes seemed close at hand, and the glaciers gleamed in the last light with a cold desolation that was in keeping with the great spaces above.

It is rarely in life that we can climb beyond the world, unburdened by personal hopes or fears, and confront the infinite facing outwards to the universe rather than inwards towards ourselves. The mystics attain this; and men of outstanding faith—both as a matter of course. But to commoner mortals it is only at moments of physical withdrawal and receptiveness, conditioned perhaps by the fatigues of a climb and a position of unique isolation, that such revelations are conferred. My watch from the Margherita platform that evening was such a moment; and it is something I will remember all my life.

Turning in from the world of stars, I crawled upstairs to my bunk. Alfons had warned me that I would not sleep at such a height. But I got underneath the three blankets, clad in five pullovers, my woollen pants and breeches, two pairs of stockings, gloves, and a woollen helmet; feeling profoundly replenished and calm, I dozed off to a sound sleep which was not interrupted till the guides rose at 3.45 A.M.

It was altogether too late for so long an expedition as we had in mind, but Alfons seemed to have been incommoded by the cold of the previous day, and was unwilling to venture forth into the outer air at a more reasonable hour. Nor did I find in Otto Taugwalder an ally.

We left the Margherita Hut at ten minutes to five. The conditions were perfect. Still air, no clouds, and a raging frost. The surface of the glacier was frozen hard as iron and gave an excellent footing. In a marvellously effortless rush over hard, sparkling snow we swooped down to the Lysjoch—past huge humps of folded blue-green glacier that exposed their age in line upon line of frozen strata—past icicle-fringed chasms and snow-choked crevasses—between séracs that flashed in the first red light of the risen sun, and séracs that towered blue and threatening above our way.

We donned our crampons at the Lysjoch and looked with interest at the steep, swaying crest ahead. From near Zermatt the Lyskamm appears as a gently rounded snow cake of unquestionable benignity. But now that the ridge confronted us, it was easy to see why it bore the grim nick-

name of " Menschenfresser " or " Gros mangeur d'hommes."
Thin, treacherously corniced and unsubstantial, the Lyskamm
provides a snow and ice climb of a high standard of interest.
The day we met it was a day of well-nigh perfect conditions,
and the traverse of the ridge was destined to be an unbroken
joy.

Alfons and I led, making the steps, and belaying each
other at exposed places. Our pace and the climbing varied
as the ridge set its problems or gave us easier ground to
cover. There was an infinite variety of incident and form.
Narrow, hard crests where we walked as on a tight-rope (and
scorned the " *à cheval* ") were followed by long stretches of
cutting up or cutting down the sides of corniced nodules.
I felt a hitherto unprecedented sense of mastery and confidence, and when we reached the eastern summit of the
Lyskamm my only regret was that the climb had lasted too
short a time.

By nine o'clock we were on the western summit, poised
above the fifteen-hundred-foot slope to the Felikjoch. Parts
of this descent are precipitous. But the snow conditions
were so beautiful that one could strike out boldly at great
speed and trust the feet. Each cramponed foot fell " Ploof! "
onto the slope, and streams of icy particles went hissing on
in front. The give of every footstep was a foot or more,
and when one achieved the right rhythm the effortless rapidity
of movement gave almost the sensation of flying. In twenty
minutes we were sitting on the Felikjoch waiting for our
companions. Alfons told me he had known the slope to
take as long as two hours or even three, when conditions
were different.

We lunched on the level expanse of the Joch, on snow

that had started rapidly to deteriorate. By the time we began attacking Castor, we were sinking in at each step. Mists came racing up from the south and the wind blew gustily as we fell into the slow rhythm of ascent.

We reached the top of Castor—that snow-white mermaid of a mountain—at eleven o'clock in the morning, and rested on its summit for half an hour while the argument went back and forth on the question of continuing over Pollux and the Breithorn, or turning back via the Zwillings Glacier. The guides were strongly for the latter, and as they stood thereby to lose financially, I became convinced in the end that Alfons was right and that we would get bogged down in the snow behind the Breithorn. To descend Castor and climb Pollux was a dead end, as the return would lie back over Castor. So the big tour was called off. We rested on our laurels.

The Zwillingsgletscher was in poor condition. Avalanches had been falling the day before and the route was tangled with a rubble of ice-blocks. The leaning séracs and hanging edifices of ice round us were built on a gigantic scale. We flitted past this menacing frozen landscape and came quickly to the lower glacier, where a maze of crevasses blocked the way. Here a grilling heat assailed us. To get below the three-thousand-metre contour after the heights we had been at, seemed like entering a hothouse. The snow was melting and the bridges were rotten, flimsy structures that fell smoking at a touch to unseen depths below. We pursued a devious and intricate route with many doublings back. Sometimes where the ice was exposed we took broad leaps across an intervening gulf, and landed with a satisfying crunch of crampon prongs on the opposite bank ; or a delicate snow-bridge had to be crossed with small light steps. Directed by Alfons, I was leading the way, and twice fell through a bridge, to feel my legs dangling over nothing ; but with axe and rope the matter was quickly rectified.

We came in the end to the dry part of the glacier. Our troubles were now over. The friendly expanses of the Grenz-gletscher awaited us, and at quarter to four we had crossed it and were sitting on the Rotenboden path undoing the ice-claws. Our tour had drawn to its close.

Looking back, I felt it to have been in many ways the most satisfying of all my mountain voyages. If it lacked the first vital and unrepeatable *élan* of the Matterhorn, it had included a notable climax, and given for the first time a sense of mastery over the environment. It marked perhaps the end of my Alpine novitiate.

III

In the pages which precede I have looked back down the avenue of the decades, almost to the beginning of the path, and then travelled forward from my earliest years to the present, trying also to take the reader on the same journey.

Gazing ahead into the uncertain future of later existence I look once again to the mountains to provide the completest expression of life. For there is no other pursuit which enables its followers to experience the fulfilment in use of all the human faculties : physical, artistic, and spiritual.

One of the best things about climbing is that anyone can do it, and at any age. It requires no special physique. It is the appanage of neither the young nor the exceptionally strong. Easier by far to make a start on than ski-ing or riding,

Dolomite washing

it is also less strenuous than most sports, and demands more modest qualifications. Its enjoyment depends less upon the subject's degree of pre-eminence than upon his attitude of mind.

If we consider the physical rewards of the mountain day we will probably agree that there are few activities, if any, which confer such a feeling of health and supreme fitness. The whole complex of muscles in the organism springs into use. The legs lift one upwards towards the skies. Lungs are filled with the exhilarating air of the heights—that sparkling air which purifies the blood and seems to lighten the weight of the body at every breath, until the human machine reaches its maximum of purposive and co-ordinated working.

And all the time the mountaineer's senses, his æsthetic and artistic faculties, are taking in the beauties round him. His to enjoy, and his alone, are the visions of rock and snow, glittering ice and lofty summit ; the evanescent patterns of cloud and sunshine on a ridge ; the solemnity of evening and the tenderness of dawn on high hills. Things undreamt of by the plainsman are unfolded in ever-changing combinations of loveliness before his eyes. Like the musician, he can inhabit a world of rhythms inaccessible to the layman. And the melody of movement is counterpoint to the harmonies of sight. The climber strives after greater skill, in a quest whose goal is never reached ; he seeks, and partially attains, the rhythm to surmount with grace every varied incident and obstacle, so that eventually some of the artistic excitement of the dancer comes to be his own.

It is in the world of the spirit, though, that the mountaineer receives his deepest satisfaction. There is nothing more refreshing during our hurried lives in this uneasy age than occasionally to take time out and withdraw from the world—to pause from the rush and turmoil of existence. The person who reaches the high ridges knows how different a viewpoint on life is achieved amid the hills, how restorative the change from pettiness and mundane cares to the pure serenity of the mountains. We enjoy there, for a time, a freedom as complete as it is possible to imagine, from the encroachments which modern governments make year by year on our liberty to tread this fair earth which is our heritage. On the mountains we attain self-mastery and a withdrawal from ties. Complete independence is temporarily our own ; we rely on no man, no communal institution, for shelter, food, warmth, or means of locomotion. No human edict regulates our coming or our going. In the isolation of lonely places the soul becomes liberated ; the flesh is disciplined and taught resistance to cold and tempest, to fatigue and thirst. We return to the plains purified, carrying back that hidden reserve of joy which is the solace of many a darkened hour ; and provided with courage to run the race that is set before us.

The peaks in their glory supply a challenge to the spirit. The mountaineer, because he is born that way and cannot help himself, responds with all his being—to the limit of his physical force, and to the extent of his artistic and spiritual awareness. It is a synthesis which for him no other activity can call forth. And he enjoys besides the deepest pleasures of human companionship. Nothing can unite human hearts more closely than the sentiment of feelings shared in common adventure, where each is dependent on the other, and the mental link is given material expression in the physical joining by the rope.

On the high summits the three-dimensional universe is

somehow transcended by a feeling of the fourth dimension. One has an awareness of the extension in time, of the relative duration of objects in the phenomenal world. At one end of the scale lies Man, most ephemeral of all physical things in sight ; next to him, the world of plants and trees, whose extension can assume a greater duration. Then the universe of peaks and glaciers, immeasurably further extended in time, but themselves condemned to the treadmill cycle of death and birth ; for as the forces of erosion and decay slowly wear away the peaks, so are new ranges slowly raised, on a time scale too immense for even the eye of fancy to apprehend. Finally, beyond all terrestrial scales of extension, beyond understanding, beyond imagination, lies the astral universe. We feel closest to it on mountain nights, when the constellations blaze through the clear, planetary air, bringing sharply to mind the vastness of celestial space. But we experience its nearness during the mountain day, when violent extremes, within a few feet of each other, of roasting sun and icy shade, are evidence of a lessening degree of protection in the earth's atmosphere, and of a greater proximity to the void of interstellar regions.

Awe is a feeling which the dweller in the modern city seldom experiences. And life is the lesser for its absence. The mountaineer crouches under the thunder of the gale, or takes shelter from the lightnings of the sky, amid the grandeur of mighty forces. The feeling of awe overreaches him ; and with it a sense of unity with nature. At rare moments a higher awareness is given, when an apprehension of the universe takes hold of the watcher and leaves a picture fixed as by a lightning flash, which the years roll past but never efface. For man is no mere creature of his habits, no defenceless and unreasoning spectator of the earthly scene ; alone among created life he enjoys the imagination to question, the will to dare. He has the power within him to transcend his earthly bonds, and " in the dust of which he is made there is also fire, lighted now and then by great winds from the sky."

Printed in Great Britain by
WILLIAM BLACKWOOD & SONS LTD.